Albert Camus

Revised Edition

Twayne's World Authors Series
French Literature

David O'Connell, Editor

Georgia State University

TWAS 69

Albert Camus
(1913–1960)
Photograph courtesy of the French Embassy Press and Information Center,
Washington, D. C.

Albert Camus

Revised Edition

By Phillip H. Rhein

Vanderbilt University

Twayne Publishers
A Division of G. K. Hall & Co. • *Boston*

Albert Camus, Revised Edition
Phillip H. Rhein

Copyright 1989 by G. K. Hall & Co.
All rights reserved.
Published by Twayne Publishers
A Division of G. K. Hall & Co.
70 Lincoln Street
Boston, Massachusetts 02111

Copyediting supervised by Barbara Sutton
Book production by Gabrielle B. McDonald
Book design by Barbara Anderson

Typeset in 11 pt. Garamond
by Huron Valley Graphics, Inc., Ann Arbor, Michigan

Printed on permanent/durable acid-free paper
and bound in the United States of America

Library of Congress Cataloging-in-Publication Data

Rhein, Phillip H.
    Albert Camus / by Phillip H. Rhein.—Rev. ed.
        p.   cm.—(Twayne's world authors series ; TWAS 69. French
    literature)
    Bibliography: p.
    Includes index.
    ISBN 0-8057-8253-2
    1. Camus, Albert, 1913–1960—Criticism and interpretation.
I. Title.   II. Series: Twayne's world authors series ; TWAS 69.
III. Series: Twayne's world authors series. French literature.
PQ2605.A3734Z734   1989
848'.91409—dc19   89-31097
                                                            CIP

To our grandchildren

Contents

About the Author

Phillip H. Rhein chaired Vanderbilt University's program in Comparative Literature from 1966 to 1979 and the Department of Germanic and Slavic Languages and Literatures from 1976 to 1988. He is a member of MLA, ACLA, ICLA, SCLA, AATG, the Southern Humanities Conference, and Phi Beta Kappa. He served as president of SCLA and on the Executive Committees of SCLA and SAMLA. He is a member of the editorial boards of the *Comparatist* and *Studies in Interdisciplinarity*. In 1979 he held the Conquest Chair in the Humanities at the Virginia Military Institute. He is the author of *The Urge to Live,* a comparative study of Kafka and Camus; *Albert Camus,* an analysis of his works; *Comparative Literature: The Early Years,* a collection of nineteenth-century essays on the theory of comparative literature; and *The Visual and Verbal Art of Alfred Kubin.* Professor Rhein has published articles on the integration of the arts, twentieth-century mythology, and twentieth-century German, French, and American novelists, and has presented papers at national and international conferences.

Preface

On 4 January 1960 the literary world was shocked by Camus's death. He was killed instantly in an automobile accident on the highway between Lourmarin and Paris. Young, successful, and world renowned, he seemingly had everything. He was in the process of beginning writing again after the torturous creative silence that followed the award of the Nobel Prize in 1957. In his briefcase was the incomplete first draft of a new book, *Le Premier Homme* (*The First Man*), his proof that he could return to creative writing and reenter the literary world. None of the promise of this new beginning was fulfilled. We are forced to look upon an incomplete body of writing as his final statement. Yet, over a quarter of a century after his death, Camus's words speak to a new generation with the same intensity that they did to those who once acclaimed him as the most significant post–World War II writer.

Among the many reasons for Camus's popularity today is the simple truth that even in an age where ideas and ideologies are overthrown in a moment, much remains constant. Literary fashion may be fleeting, but philosophic questions about the meaning of life and death still dominate serious thought and discussion. The differences between today's problems and those of past generations are meager. During the closing months of World War II, many spent their existentialist apprenticeship in reading Franz Kafka, Jean-Paul Sartre, and Camus. In these writings they found their own complex lives of solitude, slavery, and freedom rendered intelligible. Philosophy was brought down to earth for them and the anguish they experienced was given a name and better understood. In their endless conversations they rebuilt the world—richer, more just, more sincere—where the right to pursue happiness became a living reality rather than a vague constitutional right. Never had they felt so joyous or so confident about the future of humanity.

The youth of the eighties, not quite so fresh, never so adolescent, grapple with the same intellectual problems. Reared on the truths of nuclear energy, political manipulations, oppression, food shortages, and racial tensions, they, however, cannot share their parents' confidence in the future, for they are acutely aware that the scientific progress of the years that separate them from their parents has done little to augment the value of life. Today young intellectuals seek to understand rather than rebuild the world. Although they may never sit in the smoky warmth of the Café de Flore and await the late afternoon arrival of Camus after his work at Gallimard's, if time could be recaptured, the tone of the meetings and the conversations between Camus and them would be much the same. There would be no attempt by Camus to enlist disciples, for he never conceived of himself as a master. He would listen and hope that by listening he would somehow assist in the growth of the young people's intellectual freedom. Camus believed that no one can absorb a philosophic education. Each must experience the philosopher's progress to wisdom; for without personal involvement and understanding, there can be no valid philosophic development.

More than any other, this one fact alone accounts for Camus's appeal throughout the world. His thought and his art evolve from personal thoughts and experiences to a philosophic view that corresponds to the prevailing mood today. According to Camus,

We live with a few familiar ideas. Two or three. We polish and transform them according to the societies and men we happen to meet. It takes ten years to have an idea that is really one's own—that one can talk about. This is a little discouraging, of course. But we gain from this a certain familiarity with the splendor of the world. Until then, we have seen it face to face. Now we need to step aside to see its profile. A young man looks the world in the face. He has not had time to polish the idea of death and nothingness, even though he has gazed on their full horror.[1]

The "few familiar ideas" investigated and developed by Camus gradually evolved into an art and thought that were undeniably his own. The purpose of this book is to introduce the reader to Camus's art and thought as they are developed in his major writings. The book does not, however, pretend to analyze every aspect of this development. His dramatic adaptations and his journalistic writings are not discussed in detail, since these aspects of his work have been thoroughly studied in other critical essays and do not warrant repetition here.

Phillip H. Rhein

Vanderbilt University

Acknowledgments

Frontispiece courtesy of the French Embassy Press and Information Center, Washington, D.C.

Photographs of the Van Eycks' Ghent Altarpiece, St. Bavo's Cathedral, courtesy of the Belgium Tourist Office, New York.

Chronology

1939   Publication of Noces (*Nuptials*); trip to Oran.

1940   Second marriage, to Francine Faure, in Lyon; completes *L'Etranger* in May.

1941   Returns to Oran in January; completes *Le Mythe de Sisyphe* in February.

1942   Publication of *L'Etranger* (*The Stranger*) in July; leaves Algeria toward the end of 1942 to join French Resistance movement; becomes editor of clandestine newspaper *Combat*.

1942–1944   Recurrent attacks of tuberculosis.

1943   Publication of *Le Mythe de Sisyphe* (*The Myth of Sisyphus*); first "Lettre à un ami allemand" ("Letter to a German Friend"); becomes an editor at the Gallimard publishing house in Paris, a job he holds until his death.

1944   Continues as editor of *Combat* after the Liberation; production of *Le Malentendu* (*The Misunderstanding*) in Paris; second "Lettre à un ami allemand"; meets Jean-Paul Sartre.

1945   Birth in Paris of the Camus twins, Catherine and Jean; production of *Caligula;* writes *Remarque sur la révolte* (point of departuree for *L'Homme révolté*).

1946   Completes *La Peste* (*The Plague*); makes lecture tour of the United States.

1947   Publication of *La Peste.*

1948   Trip to Algeria; production of *L'Etat de siège (State of Siege*); writes "Ni victimes ni bourreaux" ("Neither Victims nor Executioners").

1950   Voyage to South America from June to August; production of *Les Justes* (*The Just Assassins*) in December; publication of *Actuelles I;* renewed attacks of tuberculosis from 1949–51.

1951   Publication of *L'Homme révolté* (*The Rebel*); controversy with Sartre.

1952   Break with Sartre in August; works on the unfinished novel *Le Premier Homme* (*The First Man*), the short stories of *L'Exil et le royaume* (*The Exile and the Kingdom*), an unfinished drama *Don Juan,* and an adaptation of Dostoevski's *Possessed.*

1953   Publication of *Actuelles II;* production of adaptations of *La Devoción de la cruz* by Calderón de la Barcas, and *Les Esprits* by Pierre Larivey.

1954   Trip to Italy in November; publication of *L'Eté*.

1955   Adaptation of *Un cas intéressant* of Dino Buzzati; trip to Greece in May; writes for Parisian newspaper *L'Express* until February 1956.

1956   Trip to Algeria; publication of *La Chute (The Fall)*; production of adaptation of William Faulkner's *Requiem for a Nun (Requiem pour une nonne)*.

1957   Publication of *L'Exil et le royaume (Exile and the Kingdom)* in March; adaptation of Lope de Vega's *Chevalier d'Olmedo* in June; receives the Nobel Prize for literature in October (the ninth and the youngest Frenchman to receive it).

1958   Publication of *Actuelles III;* trip to Greece; buys home in Lourmarin.

1959   Production of his adaptation of Dostoevski's *Possessed (Les Possédés)*; appointed director of the new state-supported experimental theater by André Malraux.

1960   Killed in automobile accident 4 January.

Chapter One

The Algerian Summer

Camus and His Time

To speak of Albert Camus and his time is to separate two entities that are essentially one. As an artist he could neither turn away from his time nor lose himself in it. If he had turned away from the breakdown of values, the struggle for power between nations, or the anxieties of sentient men and women, he would have spoken in a void. But, conversely, insofar as he took his time as his object, he asserted his own existence as subject and could not give in to it altogether. In other words, at the moment he chose to share the fate of all, he asserted the individual he was. And he could not escape from this ambiguity. "The artist," he wrote, "takes from history what he can see of it himself or undergo himself, directly or indirectly—the immediate event, in other words, and men who are alive today, not the relationship of that immediate event to a future that is invisible to the living artist."[1]

Because Camus was aware that people are "subject to history," he was able to speak for all in a common language that illuminated "the problems of the human conscience in our time." In 1957 the Nobel Prize was awarded to him in recognition of both his creative writing and his essays.[2] The latter were written concurrently with his novels and plays, and in both he explored the themes of war, resistance, executions, and exiles; the tragedies of Algeria and Hungary; the arguments for and against the death penalty; and the role of the artist. Read along with his novels and plays, the essays often provide a lucid commentary upon the position taken by Camus in his more widely read fiction.

To be understood, Camus must be read in entirety. Just as it is impossible to understand him divorced from his time, it is equally impossible to grasp the impact of his thought if his works are studied independently. From his earliest writings, composed as a young, impoverished student in Mondovi, Algeria, to his final collection of short stories, written when acclaimed as one of the world's greatest authors, there is a consistent development of theme. One has only to read *L'Envers et l'endroit* (*The Wrong Side and the Right Side*) and *Noces* (*Nuptials*) to see that there exist in these early works evidences of a deeper preoccupation.

This concern is also evident to a lesser degree in the posthumously published *Mort heureuse* (*A Happy Death*). According to Camus's notebooks, he worked on this novel between 1936 and 1938. Simultaneously he was writing the first version of *L'Envers et l'endroit* and the final version of *Noces*, and the book was written after he completed the first draft of the drama *Caligula*. As a novel *La Mort heureuse* is a failure. In spite of Camus's extensive efforts to restructure and rewrite, it remains a disjointed conglomeration of autobiographical fragments that never coalesce into a unified whole. Only the lyrical passages are artistically successful. The finest of them equal or surpass the creative use of language and the style of *L'Envers et l'endroit* and *Noces*. But there is little in the novel that foreshadows the mastery of form that we associate with Camus's later writings. Only the central theme of the quest for a life that is meaningful enough that death itself is happy gives the work philosophic significance and connects it with Camus's other works. Camus himself must have been aware that it was impossible for him to complete the novel successfully, for in spite of his persistent rewriting, the novel remains clumsily structured. It was eventually abandoned by Camus and in his mind was supplanted by the composition of *L'Etranger* (*The Stranger*). The books share obvious similarities in characters' names and in specific episodes; yet the contrasts between the two in plot and in structure are more striking than are any of the surface similarities. For the average reader the value of *La Mort heureuse* lies in its shortcomings, for by reading and analyzing it, we are better able to perceive Camus's artistic and philosophic development.

Camus's Evolving Thought

Noces was Camus's first published writing, and the experiences he illuminated within its four sections agreed in many ways with those expressed by other writers of his generation. His assumption that life was void of meaning, his apparent renunciation of hope, and his refusal of all mystical transcendence were merely an extension of the current philosophic view of the universe. He placed us in a world that is distinct from and foreign to our understanding and our desires, and he limited our experience by inescapable death. In this way Camus's thought moved in the same direction as that of Martin Heidegger, Karl Jaspers, or Sartre, but his association with these thinkers is not based on shared, systematically developed concepts. All of these men, including Camus, were concerned with the existential, but not all of them may be classified as existentialist philosophers. This point cannot be overemphasized. Camus frequently denied his alignment with existentialism; yet his critics and his reading public have continued to group him with this school. And in a certain sense Camus is an existentialist.

Throughout the history of Western thought, much creative thinking has been existentialist. In their attempts to evolve philosophic systems and attain universal and enduring truths, the classical philosophers all focused upon their own personal experiences and sought to understand their world and its history through these immediate experiences. Descartes's famous dictum "I think, therefore I am" is an existentialist concept, yet it is not existential in an ontological or epistemological sense. It is within this larger definition of the term *existentialist* that Camus's thought may be placed. He, as many thinkers, shared the existentialists' thesis that we exist in and are inescapably related to the world; that through our freedom of choice we are constantly in the state of becoming and consequently defining ourselves; and that death is the inevitable and final end of life. Camus, however, does not share the existentialists' tenet that human existence is void of essence. His entire thought rests on the belief in an innate human nature. The investigation of this belief and the continual evolvement of it is the positive feature of Camus's philosophy and the link that binds one work to another.

This linkage was intended by Camus. In 1951 when I asked him to comment upon the repetition of the events of *Le Malentendu* in *L'Etranger* and the description of the action of *L'Etranger* in *La Peste,* he wrote that "the story of *Le Malentendu* was in reality read in a newspaper. I introduced it in *L'Etranger* because I intended to develop it into a play. As you have correctly observed, the plot of *L'Etranger* similarly appears in *La Peste.* The intention there is not to be mysterious, but to indicate to the few attentive readers—at least, to my mind—my books should not be judged individually, but rather in the context of my whole work and its development."[3] Again in 1957 in the introduction to the limited edition of *L'Envers et l'endroit,* Camus spoke of the artist's long journeying to self-knowledge that is embodied in his successive works of art.

L'Envers et l'endroit

L'Envers et l'endroit, written in 1937, is Camus's earliest published work. The collection of five essays is a mixture of autobiography and lyrical meditation that contains no really unified argument. The title of the book hints at a theme that remains a suggestion rather than a logically concluded discussion. The essays present a search for some reconciliation between the "horreur de mourir" (loathing of death) and the "jalousie de vivre" (envy of life). The twenty-four-year-old Camus juxtaposes the riches of the sun and sea to the misery of human poverty. To him the sensual pleasures offered by the world make death tragic and horrible, and the fleeting moments of tenderness and desire poignantly reveal the fact of human loneliness. Throughout the compact volume, each instance illustrates the contrast between happiness and suffering and the fact that these two aspects are needed to intensify each other. The sun, sky, stars, and landscape along with the human beings who live within these elements are *l'envers et l'endroit* of an existence that contains both.

It was not until 1958 when Camus yielded to increasing pressure to permit a new edition of *L'Envers et l'endroit* that the essays became well known. His own dissatisfaction with the work is easily understood from a formal point of view. The separate sections are vague and artistically weak. Yet in the knowledge of Camus's later writings, these five pieces reveal his early mastery of expression and his consistent occupation with the themes of joy and despair. Later, in *Le Mythe de Sisyphe,* he turned to and emphasized the absurdity of human existence, but in 1937 he focused on the rapture of physical joy and wrote a manual of happiness in *Noces.*

Noces

Camus's second work is again a collection of descriptive essays closely related in theme to *L'Envers et l'endroit* but more carefully worked out in their conclusion. All four of the essays are set in the Mediterranean world that never ceased to influence Camus's literary and philosophic writings. The sun, the sea, Florence, and Algiers remain easily recognizable entities; but in Camus's handling, these images become charged with a complex, intense suggestiveness, reflecting their role in his inner world.

"Noces à Tipasa," the first essay, portrays the total surrender of the self to the eternal beauty of the universe. The momentary correspondence between the individual and nature is expressed by an exalted lyrical description of the sensual delights experienced at the Roman ruins near the ancient North African village. Surrounded by lush vegetation, intoxicated by the perfumes of exotic flowers, drenched by the sun, and enchanted by the silver and white of the sea and the flaxen-blue of the sky, the ecstasy of life and harmony with the earth are intensely felt. "Toward evening," he says, "I felt a strange joy, that joy which actors know when they have played their role well. They feel in the most precise sense, that they have made their gestures coincide with those of the ideal personage they are representing; that they have participated, in some way, in a design made in advance, and which they have made come alive and beat with their own heart. That is precisely what I felt. I had played my role well" (24).

From the rhapsodic nuptials between the individual and the universe, the mood of enchantment is quickly broken in "Le Vent à Djémila." In the windswept ruins on the plateau of Djémila, he identifies with the solitude and silence of the dead city and accepts death without hope. Camus writes, "I do not like to believe that death opens onto another life. For me it is a closed door" (35). It is here in Djémila that he obstinately refuses all the future promises of the world and clings to the richness of the present: "Everything that is proposed to me endeavors to take away from man the weight of his own life. And . . . it is exactly this certain weight of life that I demand and receive" (35).

"L'Eté à Alger," the third essay, describes the physical beauties of Algiers and its people who are "without religion and without idols" (60). Cast in its present, this is a race without a past or a tradition. Everything it does reveals its horror of stability and a disregard for the future. In the harsh summer sky of Algiers and in the violent and keen faces of this people, Camus finds "nothing on which to hang a mythology, a literature, an ethic, or a religion, but stones, flesh, stars, and those truths the hand can touch" (65). "Everything here suggests the horror of dying in a country that invites one to live" (63). In the midst of the sensual delight brought about by the union of men and women with the earth, Camus is aware that "everything that exalts life at the same time increases its absurdity" (67).

In the final essay, "Le Désert," Camus writes, "I admire, I admire that bond which, in the world, unites mankind, that double reflection in which my heart can intervene and dictate its happiness to the precise bounds where the world can then complete or destroy it" (102). It is in Italy in the "desert magnificent to the heart" that Camus meditates upon his conception of a happiness that affirms the dignity and value of human life in a world that remains indifferent to human desire. "And what more legitimate accord can unite man to life than the double consciousness of his desire for duration and his destiny of death? In this way one at least learns to count on nothing and consider the present as the only truth given us by grace" (94). This concluding essay of *Noces* reenforces the central theme of the collection. According to Camus, even though life ends in death and there is no transcendence, there remains the possibility of attaining a special kind of human happiness.

The Constants of Camus's Art

Although carefully selected and more clearly defined in his later writings, the constants of Camus's art and thought are discernible in *L'Envers et l'endroit* and *Noces*. First, the choice of titles is indicative of a technique that Camus employed throughout his artistic career. They, along with *L'Etranger* (*The Stranger*), *La Peste* (*The Plague*), *La Chute* (*The Fall*), *L'Exil et le royaume* (*Exile and the Kingdom*), attract the reader's attention and compel him or her to expand these titles into all-encompassing symbols for the works. *L'Envers et l'endroit* suggests a duality that is perhaps more clearly spelled out in *L'Exil et le royaume; Noces* is the marriage of these two aspects of existence, whereas *L'Etranger* is out of tune with his world; *La Peste* introduces disease and corruption within the kingdom, and *La Chute* indicates a complete severance, a fall from the state of grace. Second, the poetic luxuriance of Camus's language in these early essays remains an essential aspect of his later writings. Although *L'Envers et l'endroit* and *Noces* are intensely lyrical, Camus restrains his writings so that image and thought are fused, and emotion and reason are blended. Camus's lyrical expression of an attitude toward life later changes into an intellectual investigation of the same attitude, but the lyrical aspect is never totally absent from his writing.

The sentiment of absurdity that is later given distinct form in *Le Mythe de Sisyphe,* as "the divorce between man and his life, between the actor and his setting," is investigated on a personal level in these early essays.[4] In the midst of his enjoyment of the sensual delights of the natural world, Camus is aware of the tragic implications of that moment. By definition the intensity of the experience cannot endure. Men and women are born and they die. It is between these two knowns that the "present riches" must be discovered. The exaltation of the natural world and the complete refusal of the "later on" that are expressed in *Noces* form the core of Camus's thought. The fleeting pleasures of the sun's warmth, the joys of swimming, the tranquillity of the cool Mediterranean evenings that give a precious feeling of communion with the world are contrasted with the immortality and indifference of nature. The Algerian summers will succeed one another in an unending procession; and although the enjoyment of these summers may infinitely endure, the tragic fact remains that each individual's enjoyment is limited in time. The truth of human transience as opposed to the desire for permanence is one of the major philosophic themes underlying *Noces*. *Noces* is Camus's manual of happiness, and the intensity of the physical joy it describes increases the awareness of the absurd.

The problem raised by the personal atheism developed in these early essays involves a dual truth. On an abstract philosophic level there is the fact of the desire for life as opposed to the inevitability of death, but on an uncomplicated personal level there is the overwhelming earthly happiness found within this tragic framework. In "Le Désert" Camus describes how he wandered in the cloisters of Santissima Annunziata and read the inscriptions to the dead. As night was falling, he sat at the foot of a pillar and alone "was like someone seized by the throat, who shouts out his faith as if it were his dying words. Everything in me protested against such a resignation. 'You must accept,' said the tombstones. No, and I was right to rebel. I must follow this joy that goes indifferent and absorbed as a pilgrim upon this earth, must follow it step by step" (88–89). Although the tombs told him that his revolt was meaningless and that he must acquiesce to death, this proclamation had no relevance to Camus. To him, what was real was experienced; and through his revolt, his denial of sin, and his rejection of eternal life, he gained a greater intensity of life and a possibility for happiness.

By refusing to accept the religious solution to mortality, Camus renounced hope in the usual sense of the word. He did not, however, accept the equation of refusal with resignation. "To live is not to be resigned" (69). Camus asked that we, in our conscious certainty of death without hope, refuse the world but not renounce it. To accept the transience of life rather than renounce it in favor of eternal salvation is to refuse resignation. Camus reflected upon hope and our defenselessness before death in "L'Eté à Alger": "From Pandora's box, where swarmed the evils of humanity, the Greeks left out hope after all the rest as the most terrible of all. I do not know of a more moving symbol. For hope, contrary to what is believed is equivalent to resignation. And to live is not to be resigned" (69). Camus's renouncement of hope does not negate the possibility of happiness. Happiness results from oneness with the universe. The individual accepts mortal destiny and attains a happiness that is an affirmation of the dignity and unique value of existence. Within the closing pages of *Noces,* Camus presents another crucial point in his thinking. The happiness that is held forth is as brief and as fleeting as life itself; yet he asks, "What have I to do with imperishable truth, even were I to desire such a thing? It is not made to my measure. To desire it would be to deceive myself" (100).

It is only after concluding the entire collection that one understands the meaning of the seemingly pessimistic opening quotation from Stendhal's *Chroniques italiènnes:* "The executioner strangled Cardinal Carrafa with a silk cord which broke: twice he had to try again. The Cardinal watched the executioner without deigning to utter a word." The description of the encounter between the cardinal and his executioner illustrates the central point of the essays. We, like the cardinal, know our fate; but also like the cardinal, in full knowledge of our inevitable deaths, we do not cry out futilely.

The End of Camus's Algerian Summer

Camus never again knew the complete harmony with the world that he expressed in *Noces.* With the advent of World War II, his Algerian summer ended. In place of his natural gods of the sun, the sea, and the night, he was forced into the world of barbed-wire fences, tyranny, and war.[5] In September 1939 Pascal Pia appointed him editor-in-chief of the *Soir Républican.* After the paper was forced to close in January 1940 because of violations of censorship regulations, Pia secured a position for Camus as a rewrite man for the *Paris Soir.* In Paris Camus gained the experience that prepared him for the editing and disseminating of the clandestine newspaper *Combat* during the Nazi occupation of France. It was also in Paris that he was introduced to the prevalent intellectual atmosphere of France. Sartre's insistence that a writer could no longer avoid the moral responsibility for acts and attitudes inspired by his or her books reenforced Camus's own belief that the artist is obliged to bear witness to the basic rights of freedom and justice in the face of history.

In his preface to the 1959 edition of Jean Grenier's *Les Iles,* Camus wrote that it was Grenier who showed him that the light and the splendor of bodies were beautiful, but that they would perish and that we must therefore love them with the urgency of despair. "For a yong man brought up outside traditional religions, this prudent, allusive approach was perhaps the only way to direct him toward a deeper meditation on life. . . . I had to be reminded of mystery and holy things, of the finite nature of man, of a love that is impossible in order to return to my natural gods one day, less arrogantly. [Thus I owe Grenier] a doubt that will never end."[6]

Although according to Camus, it was Grenier who turned him from an unreflective life to one of meditation, it was Paris during the war years and the acclaim he received there after the publication of *L'Etranger* late in 1942 and *Le Mythe de Sisyphe* early in 1943 that brought about the dramatic change in his life. With the triumph of his writings came the end of his Algerian summer on the personal level, but the ideas that stem from his life in his native land remained constants in his later art and thought. They were modified, emphasized, or underplayed depending upon the point Camus wished to convey, but they are always there, distinguishing his writings from most of his contemporaries.

Chapter Two
The Absurd
Publication of *L'Etranger* and *Le Mythe de Sisyphe*

Immediately following World War II, *L'Etranger* (*The Stranger*) and *Le Mythe de Sisyphe* (*The Myth of Sisyphus*) were the most frequently discussed works by Camus. This popularity is readily understood. These two books corresponded to the atmosphere that permeated Nazi-occupied France at the date of their publication and have continued to address questions raised since the war. With the daily threat to humanity that existed amid the European disaster of the 1940s, it was difficult to believe in either eternal values or naive optimism, and everyone was regularly made aware of the value of a single human life. In this time when no one could afford to exist passively, Camus's fictive portrayal and philosophic account of the absurd hero expressed the uncertainty of the war-conscious Europeans, and Camus, along with Sartre, became the voice of an anxiety-ridden people. The reason for the continuation of the books' popularity into our own time needs no further comment than that implied by the horrifying news presented to us hourly by radio, television, and the newspaper.

Following the publication of both books, the identification of Camus with the absurd heroes of *L'Etranger* and *Le Mythe de Sisyphe* created a problem for the author that persisted for several years. Given the time in which they appeared, it was perhaps inevitable that the call to happiness—the positive side of Camus's work—was ignored. The appeal of his writing resulted mainly from the description of the incoherent world that he experienced, but this aspect of the works represented only one aspect of his purpose for writing. His aim from the beginning was to examine and not to proffer the philosophy of the absurd. In 1950 Camus was sufficiently distressed by his identification as a philosopher of the absurd that he wrote in "L'Enigme" that his primary concern in *Le Mythe de Sisyphe* was to examine the logical basis and intellectual justification of the "absurd sensibility" as he found it expressed in contemporary philosophy. As late as 1955, for the American edition of

Le Myth de Sisyphe, Camus again asserted that this essay marked for him "the beginning of an idea." Both of these statements reiterate a brief introductory remark for the original publication of the essay. There Camus wrote that his purpose was to "deal with an absurd sensitivity . . . and not with an absurd philosophy."

Relation of *Le Mythe de Sisyphe* to Camus's Other Writings

We are again, then, dealing with the personal development of an idea. Unlike Sartre, Camus was not a professionally trained philosopher, and he consequently spoke more as an involved individual than as an objective metaphysician. Following *L'Envers et l'endroit* and *Noces, Le Mythe de Sisyphe* may be read as an expansion of an emotional experience of life in a more rational and philosophic manner. The personal happiness that Camus had discovered in *Noces* through his acceptance of both the physical joys and the transience of existence is here analyzed in its broader implications. In *Noces* Camus found that all of his idols "have feet of clay" (102); in *Le Mythe de Sisyphe* he no longer searches for "gods of light and idols of mud" but feels a need "to find the middle path leading to the faces of man" (103).

This emotional need led Camus to explore the manifold problems that people encounter in their daily lives. The intellectual malady brought about by the contradiction between thought and experience, mind and feelings, intentions and possibilities that is universally experienced by thinking men and women initiates an emotionally understandable search for a reason for living. The essay begins with a consideration of the one truly serious problem of "judging whether life is or is not worth living." According to Camus, the answer one gives involves "the fundamental question of philosophy" (3). At the outset of Camus's investigation, the learned and classical dialectic is sacrificed to a more modest attitude of mind based upon common sense and understanding—upon the relationship between individual thought and suicide. Characteristic of Camus, the understanding of the world involves the reduction of that world to a human dimension; for a world that can be explained even with bad reasons is a familiar world and one in which people can survive. It is at the moment an individual becomes divorced from his or her life and feels an alien in a universe divested of illusion and light that the question of

suicide arises, and it is at this moment that an awareness of the feeling of
the absurd begins.

The Feeling of Absurdity

In an attempt to define this feeling of absurdity, Camus enumerates
the various ways in which the absurd manifests itself. In certain situations when asked what one is thinking, it is not unusual to become
suddenly aware of an "odd state of soul . . . in which the chain of daily
gestures is broken, in which the heart vainly seeks the link that will
connect it again" (12). Just as this experience may give rise to the
absurd feeling, so too is it possible, for no specified reason, that in the
midst of the normal monotony of the Monday through Saturday, work-
a-day world, one stops and questions the meaning of his or her routine
and "everything begins in that weariness tinged with amazement" (13).
Camus emphasizes the significance of the word "begins," for the weariness that comes from leading a mechanical life may initiate our conscious minds to think of ourselves in relationship to time. Once having
acknowledged the place of self in time, our logical thought processes
will then lead us to think about ourselves with respect to death. And
death is the most overpowering evidence of the absurd.

Intellectual Basis for the Absurd

Aware of the emotional manifestations of the absurd, Camus searches
for an intellectual basis for his feeling. From a brief investigation of the
history of science, he learns that scientific truth can only explain the
world through the enumeration of phenomena. The mind can neither
explain nor comprehend either the universe or the individual through
whom it operates. In psychology as in logic, there are truths but no
truth. Since the beginning of time the human mind has longed for a
real and rational explanation of the world, but it is forced to admit that
it cannot find such an explanation. All of the knowledge on the earth
gives us nothing to assure us that the world is ours.

The Truth of Absurdity

From the emotional and intellectual awareness of the fact of death in
contrast to the potent desire for immortality, Camus derives the truth
of absurdity. In simple terminology, the absurd always involves a

contradiction between two perceptions.] Here that contradiction exists between our longing for eternity and the inevitability of our death. It is the confrontation between the desire and the reality—neither the one nor the other in itself—that is the absurd. "[T]he feeling of the absurd becomes clear and definite. I said that the world is absurd, but I was too hasty. This world in itself is not reasonable, that is all that can be said. But what is absurd is the confrontation of this irrational and the wild longing for clarity whose call echoes in the human heart. The absurd depends as much on man as on the world" (21). For the moment, then, we experience the absurd as the unique and vital link between the world and us. And through the absurd we know what we desire, what the world offers, and what unites us with the world.

Limitations of Past Philosophies of the Absurd

From the recognition of the truth of the absurd as the result of the clash between our demand for an explanation and the mysterious evasiveness of existence, it is necessary for Camus to ascertain if thought is possible under these conditions. He turns to the writings of Heidegger, Jaspers, Lev Shestov, Søren Kierkegaard, and Edmund Husserl, and in them he finds a common recognition of an absurd universe and a basic relationship between his thoughts and theirs. He recognizes, however, that once faced with the absurd none of these philosophers remains true to it. All of them eventually destroy it by deifying the contradiction between human need and the unreasonable silence of the world. They take an unjustifiable leap into an irrationality to resolve the antinomy between human beings and the world. In every case this explanation is forced and of a religious nature. Whatever the method employed, the religious philosopher proffers a solution that, because of its rational incomprehensibility, is beyond the reach of human reason. According to Camus, for the absurd mind there is nothing beyond reason; therefore the attitude of these men, which tends to the eternal, unjustly dismisses the absurd and alters the nature of the problem. The absurd cannot be transcended, for it requires no other universe than our daily world, our earth, our fellow human beings, and ourselves. By its nature, the mystical-religious interpretation of the philosophers under discussion has neither met nor solved the question raised by the absurd. The acceptance of their ideas constitutes philosophic suicide, for these philosophers retreat from that which the mind has brought to light.

Camus's search for truth involves his personal need to understand the world and to find a unity in it that can form the basis for a meaningful life. He discovers through investigation of historical and contemporary philosophic thought that the unity he so desperately desires can only be brought about if its affirmer makes his or her judgment from without. Once a person moves outside the unity, he or she affirms an exception to it and ends in a state of contradiction. If one part of the whole is removed, then there is no whole. Neither the deification of the absurd by Jaspers and Kierkegaard, nor Shestov's identification of it with God, answers Camus's immediate need to explain the contradiction between his desire for clarity and unity and the world's irrationality, disunity, and fragmentation. Camus accepts the truth of the absurd and maintains that he must follow this truth in all its consequences.

The Burden of the Absurd

Since he cannot remain faithful to the absurd by an escape through a philosophic leap, he is forced to take upon himself the burden of the absurd through which he learns not to hope and in which he remains in continual revolt against the world. Revolt is the first of three consequences that result from the total acceptance of the absurd. Revolt is a constant confrontation between the individual and his or her obscurity, and demands an ongoing struggle with the absurd. It challenges the world every moment and it extends awareness to the whole of experience. "It is that constant presence of man in his own eyes. It is not aspiration, for it is devoid of hope" (54). Revolt gives life its value and its majesty, for it creates the beauty of the human mind at grips with a reality that exceeds it.

The second consequence of the absurd is freedom. It is not the usual conception of freedom as a condition granted by God or some higher being. Through the privation of hope and future that the absurd implies, the individual is granted an infinitely greater freedom of action. He or she is no longer concerned with the "somedays" of the future, for death is there as the only reality. In the absurd revelation the ordinary person realizes that insofar as life is planned on the basis of the future, it will conform to given goals that seem to be, but are not, a part of a nonexistent greater meaning. The absurd, however, in its denial of a future, offers an independence and a freedom that the human heart can experience and live. "The absurd man thus catches sight of a burning and frigid, transparent and limited universe in which nothing is possi-

ble but everything is given, and beyond which all is collapse and
nothingness. He can then decide to accept such a universe and draw
from it his strength, his refusal to hope, and the unyielding evidence of
a life without consolation" (60).

The third consequence of the absurd is a passion to exhaust that
which is provided by the present moment. In an absurd universe each
moment is precious, for the individual is constantly aware of approach-
ing death. "The present and the succession of presents before an ever
conscious mind, this is the ideal of the absurd man" (63–64). Each of
us must be conscious of our choices, decisions, and actions, for only
through awareness can we live up to our maximum potential.

As a result of his search for truth in a world that offers no hope and
no illusions, Camus derived the three consequences—revolt, freedom,
and passion. He transformed the invitation to death that opened the
essay into a rule of life, and he demonstrated the incomprehensibility of
human life in order to refute the senseless conclusion that it is therefore
meaningless. "Hitherto, and it has not been wasted effort, people have
played on words and pretended to believe that refusing to grant a
meaning to life necessarily leads to declaring that it is not worth living.
In truth, there is no necessary common measure between these two
judgments" (8). The value of life is enhanced by the awareness of the
impossibility of reducing it to human understanding, and in the pages
that follow, Camus gives examples of the absurd man who has accepted
the conclusions of his argument.

Four Examples of the Absurd Man

Through his choice of the seducer, the actor, the conqueror, and the
artist, Camus limits himself to men, who by the nature of their lives,
illustrate the "passion to exhaust everything that is given." In his
description of these four men, he presents each as conscious of the fact
that his activity is useless. Neither the Don Juan who receives the same
joy from each new woman he seduces, nor the actor who shares the life
of each character he portrays, nor the conqueror who acts from fascination, nor the artist (the most absurd of all) who creates has any illusions
about a life hereafter. Each seeks momentary happiness and nothing
further. There is no attempt or hope to solve the problems of human
existence. And it is this honesty toward life, this consciousness of the
uselessness of their lives that has given them their freedom and their
happiness. "Outside of that simple fatality of death, everything, joy or

happiness, is liberty. A world remains of which man is the sole master" (117). In this world existence is of infinite value because it is finite. It is a world without God in which destiny is a human affair and in which consciousness of this fact is an invitation to happiness.

Sisyphus

In the concluding passage of *Le Mythe de Sisyphe,* Sisyphus is seen as the incarnation of the absurd hero. Sisyphus, like the absurd men, hated death and the gods and was passionately attached to life. According to legend, he, the favored of mortals, was accused of having an attitude of levity toward the gods and as a result of his actions was condemned to Hades. Later he obtained Pluto's permission to return briefly to earth in order to chastise his wife for having cast his unburied body into the middle of the public square. Once again among the sun, warm stones, and the sea of the world, he no longer wished to return to Hades. So enraged were the gods that they sent Mercury to lead Sisyphus back to the underworld. For eternity he was condemned to roll a boulder to the crest of a mountain and then watch it crash back to the bottom.

It is the moment in which Sisyphus watches the stone roll down the mountainside that interests Camus. It is during that return downward to resume his torment that Camus imagines Sisyphus to have his hour of consciousness. It is a consciousness of the extent of his own misery; of the recognition of his eternal destiny. But in this moment of recognition Sisyphus transforms his torment into his victory, for he realizes that he is without hope and without power. Through his insight into the truth, he becomes superior to his destiny, for he has seen it for what it is and has become his own master. At that instant when Sisyphus returns toward his rock, he contemplates the series of unrelated actions that were created by him and combined in his memory to become his fate and to be sealed by his death. Convinced of the wholly human origin of all that is human, he endures and goes on. Camus states, "I leave Sisyphus at the foot of the mountain. One always finds one's burden again. But Sisyphus teaches the higher fidelity that negates the gods and raises rocks. He too concludes that all is well. This universe henceforth without a master seems to him neither sterile nor futile. Each atom of that stone, each mineral flake of that nightfilled mountain, in itself forms a world. The struggle itself toward the heights is enough to fill a man's heart. One must imagine Sisyphus happy" (123).

The essay concludes with this optimistic portrayal of Sisyphus. Void of hope, he nevertheless finds life so fully satisfying that he is content to spend it in his eternal struggle to the heights. Through his conscious-ness of the world without the chance of appeal to any transcendental value, he has discovered a happiness that springs from despair, and he has learned that the most appalling truths lose their power once they are recognized and accepted. The attitude exemplified by Sisyphus is alien to any possible form of physical or philosophic suicide.

Evaluation

The ideas in *Le Mythe de Sisyphe* are the result of Camus's ever evolving attempt to understand the complex realities of human experi-ence. At this point in Camus's development, the absurdist doctrine has been carried to its limits. The passive estrangement that men and women suffer in the face of the absurd will later be expanded and transformed into a new line of reasoning, but for now all we know is that our world is without God or fixed values. These ideas are tested in Camus's later creative works as he attempts to discover whether or not human dignity can persist in a world of unlimited freedom. The devel-opment of the absurd experiment explores more intently an essential dimension of human experience that opposes and supersedes the ab-surd. This dimension, which Camus labels revolt, is already defined in a limited sense in *Le Mythe de Sisyphe* as the individual's need for unity and coherence. But the reader of this essay is left with a vague and unsatisfactory sense of Camus's exact meaning of the concept.

To a degree, Camus's experiment in *Le Mythe de Sisyphe* is but another in a long line of similar processes. The experience of the absurd is certainly not peculiar either to Camus or to twentieth-century reason-ing. Friedrich Nietzsche, of course, poetically provided the classical formulation of the Death-of-God theme, but as early as 1822 G. W. F. Hegel had spoken of the infinite pain of God's absence; and such comments as André Gide's "I am convinced that God is not," or Paul Valéry's "Man thinks, therefore I am, says the Universe," or Gustav Flaubert's "Suppose the absurd were true?" all reflect the historical development of humanity trying to learn to do without God. What sets Camus's ideas apart is the fact that this book presents an experiment in thought and not an unqualified attitude or philosophic position. This type of experimental philosophy is unprecedented and emphasizes the importance Camus placed on the idea of development. He could not, or at least did not, proceed through induction to construct a consistent interpretive scheme of the universe. He chose to progress through personal involvement with the universe to an understanding of it that is humanly acceptable and definable in human terminology. It is the human element, which consistently enters into Camus's thought, that prohibits the possibility of a strictly systematic approach to any single piece of his writing. It might be said that Camus thought aloud through his writings, and just as thought is a constantly evolving process, so too is his experimental philosophizing.

Again, the necessity of reading him in his entirety cannot be overemphasized. A purely literary approach to his work is almost impossible, for so many of his ideas are clarified in his philosophic writings. On the other hand, a philosophic approach is also unsatisfactory because in his particular thought process, the abstract philosophic ideas must be translated into human situations before they are completely meaningful. Through the excellence of his imagination and the magnificence of his style, Camus is able to objectify philosophic theories through a fictional situation. Although to many critics, following the lead of Sartre's explication of *L'Etranger*, the meaning of the novel is clarified through an understanding of *Le Mythe de Sisyphe*, the reverse process is also valid, for it is through the actions of Meursault that the philosophic ideas contained in this essay take on vitality and significance for the average person caught in the torment of the twentieth century.

Chapter Three
Abstract Man
Reception of *L'Etranger*

Camus's *L'Etranger* (*The Stranger*) has taken its place alongside the works of William Faulkner, James Joyce, Kafka, and Fëdor Dostoevski on the bookshelves of many American students. This is not surprising, for the plot of the book, like those of many great books, ultimately raises more questions than it answers. It involves the reader in the final determination of the plot, and forces him or her to resolve the conflict between Meursault's seeming innocence and the uncontested fact that he murdered another man. The novel is simply and beautifully written, and once it is in the hands of inquiring students, its power and enigmatic nature stimulate further thought. Although *L'Etranger* may be the students' initiation to philosophic concepts that they do not fully comprehend, this story of a man who is executed for having smoked at his mother's wake arouses their intellectual curiosity and initiates a never-ending chain of questions about the meaning of life.

Barring the praise the book has received for its structure, beauty of language, and philosophic content, the unquestionable popularity that it has enjoyed is valid proof of its significance. *L'Etranger* was published in 1942 when Camus was twenty-nine. He was in Paris at the time, but the fact that the novel's conception stems from the emotional and intellectual climate of his life in Algeria may partially account for its appeal to the present generation. Like many young Americans today, the Camus of Algiers had experienced neither the ravages of a war nor the sophisticated climate of a large European city. Conversely, again like many Americans, he was aware of the newness and originality of his country and of the strange and fascinating beauty of this world. It was his concern with the development of ethical values in such an environment and his intellectual need to establish a valid justification for life devoid of any transcendental definition that led him to a career as a writer, and it was his ability to express his thoughts artistically that led to the almost immediate acceptance of him as one of Europe's greatest authors.

Meursault

L'Etranger is the first internationally successful piece of writing from this period of Camus's life, and its popularity is closely related to the fact that Meursault's problems are essentially those of most young people in a predominantly bourgeois, moralistic society. Meursault's story, related in first person, must be that of a youth, for it is usually only young people who openly defy the rules of life dictated by society. Once youth has passed, the rules of the game are not easily forgotten, and those who refuse to conform to them are not readily forgiven. In the course of the novel, as we get to know Meursault's character, we are tempted to see him as irresponsible and antisocial. He acts in a human situation as if human relationships do not exist. It is a fact that he becomes enmeshed in a sordid affair involvng Raymond, an acquaintance, without ever questioning the possible outcome, and it is also a fact that he murders an Arab. We are led to believe that he is completely indifferent to everything except physical sensations. He is thirty and a bachelor, and he dutifully pursues his profession as a clerk. He is, however, more interested in the pleasant dryness of a washroom towel at midday and its clamminess at night than in a possible promotion to Paris. He lives in a succession of presents in which all pleasures are sensual experiences. Smoking, eating, swimming, and fornicating are all equal acts. Even the death of his mother has no immediate effect upon him. He is detached from any of life's usual entanglements, and he remains detached until after he murders the Arab. This change in Meursault's character from initial unawareness to an almost alarming awareness after the murder would be inconceivable if we did not also catch a glimpse of another Meursault who lived as a student in Paris and was presumably not always so passive as we find him in the first part of the book. Actually he is far from being totally deprived of passion, for it is his passion that leads him to his decision to be honest to himself and to base his life on the truth of being and feeling. And it is this decision that makes him a stranger in a society whose existence depends upon everyone's concession to its codes and rituals. According to Camus, Meursault is a man "who does not play the game. He is a man poor and naked who is in love with the sun."[1]

The Dominant Theme

The dominant theme of *L'Etranger* becomes clear in the second part of the book. The murder of the Arab is the event that binds together the disconnected succession of moments in Meursault's earlier life to make up a past that can be judged. Confined in prison and condemned to death, Meursault is forced to evaluate his relationship with the world. He is aware that society refused him the final rights of judgment and denied him his importance as an individual. He knows that the absolute religious and social values by which he was judged are conventional and outworn. He is cognizant of all this; yet in full realization of the limitations of society, his final wish is not to withdraw from it but to resubject himself to the tortuous entanglements of day-to-day living. The reason for this wish can only be explained by his one additional discovery. Near death, he learns that life with all of its irrationality is not only worth living, but that it offers him his only chance for happiness. The absurdity of life, which actually has nothing to do with either society or behavior within society, cannot be denied or eradicated. It is in reality an invitation to a happiness completely rooted in the knowledge that men and women live and they die. There are no other absolute truths. Meursault's "I, too, felt ready to start life all over again" (154) echoes Sisyphus's statement that "the struggle itself toward the heights is enough to fill a man's heart" (123).

Meursault's fight to the summit demands almost superhuman endurance, for his discovery of the singular value of life does not occur until the last pages of the novel. He is dragged through defeat after defeat before he is able to acknowledge the one glaring truth that he chose to ignore throughout the major portion of the novel. In this way *L'Etranger* is a novel of development in which the protagonist goes through the agonizing experience of moving from a basic indifference toward life to a conscious realization that the infinite value of life lies in the very finiteness of its nature. The existence Meursault had been leading is brought into question by his imprisonment and trial. He rejects the rational definition of men and women that is proffered by the legal system; he rejects suicide as an escape from life's irrationality; he affirms the value of an individual life; and finally, as a consequence of his failure to accept any philosophic system that seeks to eradicate the finiteness of existence, he recognizes the absurdity of life.

From the moment of Meursault's arrest, the world in terms of his experience becomes inexplicable to him. According to the standards by which he had conducted his life, there is no basis for his arrest. He had acted out of indifference to everything except physical sensations; and projecting this philosophy to the extreme, he saw no difference between firing and not firing the shots into the body of the Arab. With his arrest, he is abruptly introduced into a world he cannot understand. The moment of the clash between the opposed demands of his individual moral code and the social code by which he is judged initiates his gradual awakening to the absurdity of the universe.

Before Meursault acknowledges the inauthenticity of his own life, he endeavors to strike out against the society that has placed him in confinement. Characteristically, he does not actively seek an explanation for his arrest; however, his imprisonment automatically exposes him to the values devised by the law courts and the church. Neither social nor religious law can resolve the conflict within him, but since those laws are the bases for his condemnation, they are the instruments that ultimately lead him to a positive affirmation of life. In his quest for meaning, it is at the moment of imminent death that he finally turns from exterior forces inward to himself. Although he chooses to transform the world rather than conform to it, he dies knowing that he has failed. Throughout his life, he refused to question anything. Hoping to transform the world by ignoring its limitations, he accepted only the sensual aspects of life. At the time of his death he realizes for the first time that happiness cannot exist in a world where all actions are equal. He discovers that in the face of the absurd fact that everyone must die, no one can afford just to exist. To fail to question the meaning of life is to condemn the individual and the world to nothingness.

The Affirmation of Life

In *L'Etranger* Meursault is above all else a man who wants to go on living. No matter how unbearable prison life becomes for him, death is never a temptation. Life at any price is worth the living. His desire for life is most clearly expressed when he says, "I've often thought that had I been compelled to live in the trunk of a dead tree, with nothing to do but gaze up at the patch of sky just overhead, I'd have got used to it by degrees" (95). He is an ordinary man, an office clerk, with ordinary hopes and ambitions. In his thorough enjoyment of each sensual pleasure, he never thought of the time when these experiences would be ended by death. It is at the time of his arrest that he is jarred out of his feeling of complacency and is forced to think of himself in association with the world. He no longer understands the relationship between himself and the universe. Only gradually does he realize and accept the clash between his desire that the world be explicable and the fact that it is not. As a representative of everyone, he must seek out, be subjected to, and finally reject all the time-honored answers offered to solve the enigmatic relationship between the individual and the universe. In his search for a meaning to life, the one positive conclusion that Meursault finally reaches is that life is finite. Nowhere within this world can he find any proof of a life beyond the grave. He knows that he exists and that the world exists, and he becomes increasingly aware that anything beyond these two tangible facts is mere construction. He tosses about from the purely sensual to the logical to the religious, but nowhere is he able to find anything but paradox. Every new adventure reinforces the illogic of the earth. Meursault discovers but one truth concerning human existence: "A childishly simple, obvious, almost silly truth, but one that's hard to come by and heavy to endure . . . Men die and they are not happy."[2] Meursault's search for truth, unity, and meaning in life is constantly blocked by the irrational world. Finally faced with imminent death and exhausted by a fruitless battle waged in an attempt to alter the unalterable, he is forced to accept the doctrine of absurdity. He relinquishes all efforts to transcend or destroy the limitations of human existence and submits to an indifferent nature that remains forever distinct from and foreign to him.

In *L'Etranger* the acceptance of the doctrine of the absurd in no way implies disdain of the universe. Throughout the novel Meursault clings to the strange, fascinating beauty of a world that he cannot comprehend. The warmth of a female body, the odors of the sea, the brilliance of the sun are in fact what make life worth living for him. Rather than a rejection of the universe, Meursault's desire for life is deeply rooted in a total acceptance of the natural universe. What he learns through his contacts with the structures of society is that he is alone and that all of his actions are equally unimportant and insignificant in their effect upon the universe. Everyone must die, and Meursault realizes that nothing can be done to alter the course of human destiny. Finally aware of the brute facts of existence, he ceases to search for some possible escape from his fate and totally resigns himself to the grandeur of the universe. He cannot and never will understand the relationship between himself and the world, but somehow he no longer needs to understand it.

During his incarceration he also realizes that everyone is oppressed by external values that have nothing to do with the nature of either the individual or the universe. Life is ruled by outdated pretentions that should, as those who created them, be disintegrated into ashes. Meursault's recognition of the fact that societal oppression is something he can act upon is the beginning of his revolt. Although this feeling of revolt comes too late to have any positive results in his life, it is clearly formulated. By implication, in Meursault's wish that he be greeted by howls of execration at his execution, an invitation is extended toward a life freed from involvement in the outworn dictates of twentieth-century civilization. Through Meursault's failure as an individual, he brings awareness to the rest of us.⸢His entire existence was squandered in a quest for a meaning to life that he finally discovered near the time of his death⸥ This waste of human effort was, however, not only his fault but also that of a social code that made no provisions for deviations in actions. The invitation offered by Meursault is that we cease our attempt to conquer the unconquerable, that we acknowledge the absurdity of life, and that in full recognition of our limits we seek to build a society that acknowledges human dignity above all else.

The implication underlying the theme of *L'Etranger* is that a world in which God is dead and destiny is a human affair need not be an unhappy world. From the individual recognition of the absurdity of life emerges a happiness that is neither sensual nor transcendent but the affirmation of the dignity and unique value of life. In a world that offers no hope, we learn through the double consciousness of our desire for duration and our destiny of death to count on nothing and to consider the present as the only given truth. From our consciousness that we are our own end and the only end to which we can aspire, it is right for us to question, but this questioning must result in an affirmation of the world of true values. Camus's basic attack is directed against the unnecessary suffering entailed by us in our relationships with others. He pleads for recognition of the tragic journey of life and for a realization that we are not isolated. He is appalled by our blindness not only in refusing to recognize the tragedy of human life but also in refusing to see the value of acting decently. Questioning alone leads us to frustration and resultant pessimism, but this pessimism must be a point of departure that takes us out of our individual despair. The transitoriness of life is the link of solidarity we have with each other. Once we are aware that we do not have to battle alone, we can combine our forces with those of others and reestablish human dignity as the single most important measure of societal action.

Relationship of *L'Etranger* to Camus's Other Works

The character of Meursault clearly illustrates the continual development of Camus's thoughts on the absurd. Meursault not only recalls the world of *L'Envers et l'endroit* and *Noces,* but he also prepares the reader for extensions of the absurdist experiment that are analyzed in Camus's later writings. Meursault's instinctive awareness of the increased value of life brought about by the fact of mortality and his enjoyment of physical sensations recall Camus's expression of his feelings at Djémila when he said, "If I obstinately refuse all the 'later on' of this world, it is because I do not want to give up my present riches." The warmth of the sun, the cry of the boys selling iced drinks in the square, the pleasures of the beach, and the cool Mediterranean evenings are the joys that Meursault sorely misses as he lies in his prison cell, and these are the same experiences that Camus describes in *Noces* as the source of a happy life. Meursault as a man who cannot lie possesses the moral quality that Camus most admired in his fellow Algerians. In the simple pagan civilization of North Africa, people observed certain basic rules in their relationships with each other. The Algerians' feeling of communion with their fellows is an essential aspect of Meursault's character and one that gives him a dignity beyond the simple rules that society has incarnated in its laws.

The connection between *Le Mythe de Sisyphe* and *L'Etranger* is unmistakable. Although the essay analyzes our experience of the world and attempts to show the nature of the interaction between experience and world, and the novel selects certain experiences and sets them into conflict with the world, Meursault is in many ways a modern Sisyphus—although if extended beyond the obvious similar details, the analogy is stretched too far because of the difference in purpose between the novel and the essay. In *L'Etranger* Camus conveys rather than examines the absurd experience. Nevertheless, both the godlike Sisyphus and the office worker Meursault are aware of the absurd and through their awareness gain their revolt, their freedom, and their passion. Meursault's wish for cries of execration at the end of the novel expresses his recognition of the absurd and its consequences, and they illustrate on a human level the complicated reasoning of *Le Mythe de Sisyphe.*

In the dialogue between the mind and experience that Camus presents to his readers, each work contains many ideas and attitudes that he has previously developed, but each of them also introduces new concepts that sharply differentiate them from the preceding writings. The aspect of absurdity that denies that the world has coherency is one familiar to readers of *L'Envers et l'endroit* and *Noces,* and it is also experienced by Meursault; however, in *L'Etranger*—and again through Meursault—Camus introduces a broader concept of the absurd, which is less optimistic and implies that the absurdity of the world is not merely passive but is a cruel and hostile force. Meursault is not presented as an ideal example of how to live in an absurd universe, but Camus does offer him as an example of a person who becomes aware of such a universe, who suffers because of it, struggles against it, and is finally defeated by it. It is at the point of defeat that the question of Meursault's innocence arises. There is no doubt that he committed a detestable act in his murder of the Arab, but Camus does not condemn him. In fact, the evidence is stacked in such a way that Meursault is condemned through a misunderstanding. It is not because he killed an Arab that he is executed but because he did not weep at his mother's funeral. If Meursault is innocent, then the implication is that society incarnates a malign absurdity. The force of this aspect of absurdity is emphasized by the story of the Czech, which Meursault keeps reading over and over again in his prison cell; and although Meursault finds the story unbelievable from his point of view, it can be interpreted by the reader as a symbol of Meursault's destiny. Just as the son in the story, Meursault is also a victim of a kind of intangible fate that has little to do with Camus's usual definition of the absurd. The story itself becomes the plot of *Le Malentendu,* and this particular aspect of absurdity is further examined and given dramatic form in *Caligula* and *Le Malentendu.*

It is also within these two dramas that the question of limits— hinted at in *L'Etranger*—is further clarified and investigated. In his portrayal of Meursault, Camus implies that we cannot live happily or productively if all events are thought to be morally equivalent. To Camus all actions are not equal, and they can be judged without invoking the aid of sources beyond human experience. This tenet of Camus's thought, implied here and analyzed in the dramas, concludes the absurd experiment and evolves into the philosophy of revolt.

Chapter Four

The Theater of the Absurd

Camus and the Theater

In a television interview Camus was once asked the reason for his interest in the theater. He simply replied that he was happy there. In the company of actors, writers, producers, and stage hands, he found an ambience that pleased him. As early as 1935 he was actively engaged in the cooperative *Théâtre du Travail* in Algiers, and it was from his experience in acting, writing, and directing in this group and in the later organized *Théâtre de l'Equipe* that he developed his dramatic theories. Through their dependence on each other and their mutual struggle toward a well-defined end, the members of the acting companies created a community of solidarity. Within this community Camus was able to experiment freely and creatively with ideas, language, and dramatic theory.

As might be anticipated, Camus used the theater as a medium for serious statements about life. Most outstanding writers of the twentieth century have attempted to reflect current moral and philosophic problems in their works, and in this respect Camus's intent is similar to that of such French, Swiss, and American playwrights as Jean Anouilh, Sartre, Max Frisch, Friedrich Dürrenmatt, and Tennessee Williams. The similarities, however, between Camus's dramas and those of these other authors are limited. They all wrote plays that consider the doubts and aspirations of their times, that discuss serious themes, and that portray fundamental emotions; but the choice of themes and the manner in which they are developed varies with each author.

Theory of Tragedy

As a playwright Camus mainly thought in terms of tragedy, for he felt that the audience's involvement was most intense in this form of drama. He neither admired a theater such as that of Berthold Brecht, which consistently sought to criticize moral or social evils, nor was he

27

satisfied with the drama developed by his brilliant French predecessors. He denounced the ornate, diffuse language of Jean Giraudoux and the alien Catholic universe of Paul Claudel. In his search for a personally more satisfying type of dramatic expression, Camus studied Greek and Renaissance history to try to find the reason for the tremendous dramatic output in those periods. He found that during these stages in the development of Western thought, individualistic attitudes evolved within what had previously been a homogeneous society; and that as a result of the emergence of new ideas, the individual who propounded them was placed in conflict with the group. Camus reasoned that if tragedy is born from this conflict between two equally strong and equally right antagonistic forces, and if the Greek and Renaissance writers created the greatest known tragedy, then it followed that if the present time possessed the same operative factors, it also was capable of stimulating the composition of great tragedy. His concept of tragedy is basically Greek, but it can also be understood in Nietzschean terms. The two conflicting forces of the individual's passionate assertion of freedom and of the will to live are juxtaposed to the irrefutable natural order, which dictates mortality. These antagonistic forces are in contention within a drama such as *Oedipus Rex*. In Sophocles' play the nearly perfect Oedipus must finally succumb to the will of the gods and admit his human limitations. Camus's experiments in twentieth-century tragedy—even though he insists that modern tragedy should be independent of and distinct from its predecessors—share the Greek tendency to portray metaphysical dilemmas rather than individualized and humanized emotions.

In his essay "Sur l'avenir de la tragédie" Camus perceives the tragic situation as the consequence of the opposition of two powers in a forced immobility.[1] One of these powers is the universe, which the Greeks personified in their gods, and the other power is the human being, personified in a hero like Prometheus who revolted against the divine order. It is essential to tragedy that each of these forces be equally legitimate. Prometheus must be justified in his revolt, but at the same time Zeus cannot be completely wrong. In a tragedy these two justifiable—yet not totally just—forces must be kept in perfect balance. Although there is no absolute right or wrong superimposed upon the contending forces in a tragedy, any given force can be right up to a certain point. The constant theme of tragedy, according to Camus, is the limit beyond which one must not go. The individual who overlooks this limit out of blindness or passion and tries to enforce a power that only he or she possesses is destined for catastrophe. To be mistaken about this limit, to try to break the equilibrium of forces, is to destroy oneself. Along the extremities of the limit, equally legitimate forces meet in "quivering and endless confrontation" (302). The outcome of tragedy must be ambiguous, for to resolve the conflict would break the equilibrium and interrupt the vibrant confrontation.

Camus believed that in ancient Greece and during the Renaissance the questioning of the established sacred orders created an atmosphere conducive to the writing of tragedy. According to Camus, a comparable intellectual attitude prevails in the twentieth century. Although twentieth-century men and women have neither the Olympian nor the Christian gods to question, today's Socrates and Descartes revolt against a universe of their own making. The world they thought could be shaped with science has become monstrous. Revolt against the cruelty of the old divine order has produced only more cruelty, and history has become as grim and implacable as destiny. Men and women, having set progress up as a god, now turn against the god they created. Thus, just as in Hellenic times and in the Renaissance, the individual stands before civilization in a state of rupture without having found something new to satisfy his or her longing. "Today man proclaims his revolt, knowing this revolt has limits, demands liberty though he is subject to necessity; this contradictory man, torn, conscious henceforth of human and historical ambiguity, is the tragic man" (307). To present this man or woman to a contemporary audience was Camus's primary reason for writing.

Le Malentendu

The Parisian audience was introduced to his dramas by the Marcel Herrand production of *Le Malentendu* (*The Misunderstanding*) at the Mathurins theater in 1944.[2] Although *Caligula* was written in 1938, *Le Malentendu* was Camus's first work to be conceived and written outside of North Africa, and it provides an excellent link to *L'Etranger*. The piece of newspaper that Meursault found in his cell while awaiting his trial contained an article about an unusual and ridiculous tragedy. A Czechoslovakian man had left his native village in order to go abroad and make his fortune. After twenty-five years he and his family returned to his birthplace. For the pleasure of a joke, he left his wife and child at an inn and without revealing his identity decided to take a room at a hotel run by his mother and sister. Neither of them recognized him, and during the night they killed him, stole his money, and threw his body into the river. When his wife arrived at the hotel on the following morning and disclosed his name, the mother hanged herself and the sister committed suicide by jumping into a well. Meursault found the story unbelievable from one point of view but, from another, quite natural—"in any case . . . one must never fool around." Jan's desire to be recognized and to find his place in the world ends as tragically as Meursault's attempt to remain uninvolved in society and indifferent to the world. And it is precisely Meursault's criticism of Jan's "fooling around" that forms the major distinction between the *fait divers* reported in *L'Etranger* and the three-act drama that Camus developed into *Le Malentendu.*

In *Le Malentendu,* the strong drive toward love and happiness is placed in conflict with an absurd universe in which everyone is irremediably lonely and all attempts at communication result in misunderstandings. By destroying the innocent men who visit their hotel, Martha and her mother reflect on a human level the impersonal order of the universe, which is challenged by and brought into conflict with Maria's and Jan's desire for recognition and happiness. Each of these forces has the double mask of good and evil. The two women are wrong to kill innocents, but their longing for an ideal world where "things are what they are" somehow justifies their actions; and even though Jan's wish to bring his family happiness is noble, his coming into his own home as a stranger is a mistake.[3] Since no limits are imposed on human action, no questions asked, no depositions made, and no verdicts given, the play ends in disaster. Jan is dead, the mother commits suicide, Martha prepares to die in isolation, and Maria is alone and desperate. The only alternative to the devastating outcome of the drama is an impossible one. If Jan had been sincere and had found the right words, all might have been saved, but given the characters and the situation presented, such an outcome is not possible. The conflict in *Le Malentendu* is resolved in favor of the universe. Human happiness becomes a matter of luck, and the solution to the absurdity of the world found in the physical life of *Noces, Le Mythe de Sisyphe,* and *L'Etranger* is shown to be impossible to those not born in a country of the sun.

The world that Martha and her mother create in their inn reflects a universe in which the frustration of love and desire is inevitable and in the natural order of things. In *Le Malentendu,* Camus implies that nowhere on earth are we able to find comfort and feel at home. The room given to Jan is to sleep in and the world is made for him to die in.

Destiny destroys the innocent in the same way that the two women victimize their guests. Although Jan is murdered through a misunderstanding, the misunderstanding is not by chance. In a universe that has no place for hope or desire, there is an order. When Maria reveals Jan's identity to Martha, Martha tells her, "so all of us are served now, as we should be, in the order of things" (132).

The lack of recognition, communication, and understanding inherent in the world is strikingly underlined by the actions of an old servant. He speaks as little as possible, and then he says only as much as he has to. He has trouble hearing, and he misunderstands what is said to him. At one time when Jan is alone in his room and is eager to escape the haunting loneliness and "the fear that there is no answer" (107), he rings for the servant. The old man appears but says nothing. Again at the conclusion of the drama, the servant comes onto the stage in answer to Maria's passionate cry to God for help. "Oh, God," she appeals, "I cannot live in this desert! It is on You that I must call and I shall find the words. . . . Have pity, turn toward me. Hear me and raise me from the dust, O Heavenly Father! Have pity on those who love each other and are parted" (133). The servant answers "No." Whether or not the old man symbolizes God is debatable, but he does reveal the painful fact that we are alone in our suffering and that any appeal to a miraculous revelation from a transcendental realm is in vain.

Caligula

The problem of suffering in a world that has no meaning is also central to the play *Caligula*. Camus uses Suetonius's story of the mad emperor to develop and subsequently reject the notion that "tout est permis" ("everything is permitted"). Like Martha and her mother, Caligula finds the world unsatisfactory, and in his attempt to refashion it by making himself equal to the gods, he, again like the two women in *Le Malentendu,* becomes an embodiment of the absurd on earth. The dramatic action begins with and is dominated by Caligula's discovery of the simple truth that "men die and they are not happy" (8). Given the unsatisfactory state of the world as it is, Caligula tries to transcend death and misery by creating "a kingdom where the impossible is king" (16). The death of his sister Drusilla has made him aware of the absurd and given him a need of "the moon, or happiness, or eternal life— something, in fact, that may sound crazy, but which isn't of this world" (8). Others have longed for the poetically impossible, but unlike them Caligula has absolute power as the emperor. He decides to use this power to create a kingdom of the impossible. It is a question, he says, of making possible that which is not possible. When the moon is in his hands and the impossible is on earth, then he and the world will be transformed. People will not die and they will be happy. His hope is that finally "when all is leveled out, when the impossible has come to earth, and the moon is in my hands—then, perhaps I shall be transfigured and the world renewed; then men will die no more and at last be happy" (17).

In his attempt to transform the world Caligula becomes an apostle of the absurd. He insists that everyone recognize the absurdity of the world. He decrees famine and execution, rewards a slave guilty of theft with the gift of a fortune because he has remained silent under torture, and he commands that the prize for civic virtue shall go to the citizen who has most often visited the state brothels. In his every act he strives to equal the gods in cruelty, stupidity, and hatred. To demonstrate his likeness to the gods, he dresses as Venus and forces the people to pray to the goddess to teach them the truth of the world. The truth he teaches is that there is no truth. In spite of the obvious ridiculousness of his actions, the logic underlying them is never questioned. The audience is constantly made aware of the fact that the world is absurd, and that Caligula's actions—no matter how seemingly wrong—cannot be condemned. There is nothing in the nature of things that can prove him wrong. The world is absurd and his actions merely underscore this overwhelming truth.

Although the rules of logic cannot destroy Caligula, he dies knowing that he has failed. His statement "I have chosen a wrong path, a path that leads to nothing. My freedom isn't the right one" (73) invites us to find the reason for his failure in something other than the laws of logic. In pursuing his reign of absurdity, Caligula acts as if his freedom were limitless, as if all actions were equal. His rule is opposed on the one hand by the patricians who uphold the sanctified social institutions and condemn the idea of absurdity in the name of the gods or eternal values, but their opposition is proved ineffectual. On the other hand, the character Cherea, Caligula's confidant, resists Caligula's reign of terror for entirely different reasons. Without seeking to defend his position from any rational or religious viewpoint, he simply states that "some actions are . . . more praiseworthy than others" (52). It is not a higher ideal that makes him oppose Caligula, but rather a personal belief that all actions are not equal and that our duty is to judge human actions and to set limits that cannot be transgressed. The world remains absurd, but Cherea introduces a concept that will not permit uncontrolled freedom to destroy basic human rights.

Caligula's error is not his rebellion against absurdity but rather his failure to recognize the limits of permissible action. By destroying Caligula's kingdom of the impossible, Camus introduces a concept that is more fully analyzed and developed in his subsequent writings. It is important to our understanding of his evolving thought to be aware that at this early date the concept of revolt and the idea of limits are adequately formulated so that Camus's switch from an emphasis on the notion of absurdity to an investigation of permissible actions in an absurd universe is apparent. In a world without God and without recourse to an absolute order, we are still not free to do whatever we please. There are inherent limits that forbid actions that ignore the rights of others. Caligula finally recognizes this fact and admits his failure. He dies knowing that he is neither innocent nor justified. His hour of death, like that of the characters of *Le Malentendu* and Meursault from *L'Etranger,* is also his hour of truth. In the dramas as well as in the novel the individuals are doomed to suffer and to die, but through their suffering they become aware of an order that limits their freedom. They realize that even though the world has no hierarchy of metaphysical values, it does have bounds that govern and limit selfish ambitions.

Relationship to Camus's Other Works

Like *L'Etranger, Caligula* and *Le Malentendu* are concerned with the moral distress of a society that can no longer reach outside itself for a coherent system of ethical values. Unlike in *L'Etranger,* however, in both *Caligula* and *Le Malentendu* a stronger emphasis is placed on a spirit of revolt against the hostile aspects of the world's absurdity than against the societal standards of morality. Camus has refused to draw the nihilist conclusion that because the world is irrational, the irrational is the only logical principle of conduct. Discovering that the world is absurd, Martha and her mother and Caligula imagine that they can somehow transform it for the better. For the mother and daughter this idea is projected into their dream of the land "where summer crushes everything," and the means that they employ to attain their dream are never questioned. Caligula inaugurates a capricious reign of terror and topsy-turvy morality in his attempt to transform the world by becoming the prophet of absolute absurdity. In his dreadful way he is awakening his subjects to the absurdity of existence, but his truth is an abstraction, and Camus seems to be saying that we cannot live by abstractions alone. This idea is later more fully developed in *L'Homme révolté,* but for the moment the readers' attention is switched from the study of ideologies that corrupt us to nature, which sobers us with reminders of our limits. Caligula is destroyed by a revolt that was prompted by the instinctive recognition that his conduct exceeded life's absurdity.

This is the rough draft of metaphysical revolt, rooted in the spirit of average men and women who have braced themselves against fate and have refused to accept it without battle. In his 1955 preface to the American edition of *Le Mythe de Sisyphe,* Camus remarked that "within the limits of nihilism, it is possible to proceed beyond nihilism." To Camus despair has always been the ultimate sin, and he argues this point in his *Lettres à un ami allenmand* (*Letters to a German Friend*). These letters to an imaginary German friend were originally published by the underground press in 1943 and 1945. They introduce a concept of revolt strikingly different from the personal attitude expressed in either *Noces* or *Le Mythe de Sisyphe.* In both of these earlier works revolt was seen as an essentially sterile notion, which aspired to nothing and was completely without hope. This is the type of revolt illustrated by the actions of Martha and Caligula in their attempts to fulfill a nostalgic longing for a reasonable world. In *the Lettres à un ami allemand,* however, Camus redefines the term in order to provide a means of escape from the private and solitary world of a Meursault or a Caligula into a world in which the individual is vitally concerned with his or her relationship with others and with society.

The most obvious reasons for this change in concept stem from Camus's experiences during the war. The events of the war vividly emphasized the interdependence of human beings, and Camus became increasingly aware of the relationship between individual happiness and the attitude and conduct of others. He saw that a world void of belief in moral principles, in which the individual was free to act in accordance with desire, could lead to a total disregard for the life and welfare of others. In opposition to absolute individual freedom, he proposed an attitude of revolt that refused to add to human misery and that actively opposed those who did so. This new connotation of the meaning of revolt expressed in the four letters is further clarified in the 1945 essay "Remarque sur la révolte," but it is adequately formulated here to give us a clear insight into Camus's changing attitude at the time he was composing *La Peste.*

Chapter Five

An Invitation to Happiness

Publication and Reception of *La Peste*

La Peste (*The Plague*) is the best known and the most popular of Camus's writings. Published in 1947, it has been translated into sixteen languages and has become one of the most widely read books published in France since World War II. There are many reasons for this positive reception; however, its almost universal appeal derives more from Camus's expression of compassion and respect for human beings than it does from any of the book's political, social, or metaphysical implications. On the surface the novel seems to mark a distinct change in Camus's philosophy; but as is so often true in a discussion about Camus, what at first appears to be a rejection of earlier ideas is later perceived as a development in or a reevaluation of his thinking. In *La Peste* there is no attempt to transform the world depicted in *Le Mythe de Sisyphe* or *L'Etranger*. The war years and the consequent human suffering made Camus aware of the inadequacy of his earlier philosophy, and in *La Peste* he switches his concern from intellectual to personal problems. Here he emphasizes the need for the fragile joys of life. The world remains absurd, but its appearance changes. Men and women discover that they are not alone, and through the knowledge that "the grocer and [they] are both oppressed" they gain the strength to resist, if not transform, the world.

Plot

La Peste is a chronicle of events that took place in the city of Oran between 16 April 194– and February of the following year. The book is divided into five major sections, which are artistically handled in such a way that both the events and the structuring of the events reveal the progress of the plague. The opening portion describes individual actions in a city as yet not officially touched by plague. The major characters are introduced and are seen doing business, arranging for journeys, and making decisions as if everything and every action were still possible. The second part of the book begins with the statement "From now on, it can be said that plague was the concern of all of us."[1] Once the town gates are shut, the individual actions, emphasized in the first part of the book, give way to the more universal feelings of fear and separation shared by all. Although the description of Rambert's various attempts to escape from Oran make up a major portion of this section, individual responses to the plague are overshadowed by an analysis of the general reactions of the people. The individual is still seen in a heartrending struggle to recover lost happiness and to balk the plague, but by the beginning of part three everyone acknowledges the fact that there are no longer individual destinies: "only a collective destiny, made up of plague and the emotions shared by all" (151). In this third section, no isolated actions are described. The individual revolt of the first weeks of the plague is supplanted by a vast despondency in which nothing is left "but a series of present moments" (165). The people of Oran now take an interest only in what interests everyone else. The deadening immobility described in part three contrasts to the vibrant descriptions of individual actions that make part four the most moving and significant section of the book. The poetic impact of the death of Othon's child, Paneloux's second sermon, and Tarrou's confession prepares the readers for the sudden and unexpected return of the rats to the city at the end of part four. The brief fifth section deals with the end of the plague, the reunion of lovers, and the return to the individual feelings and actions that made up the introductory section.

On the literal level *La Peste* has very little plot. The narrative simply follows the plague from its beginnings to its eventual disappearance, and it can be successfully and absorbingly read as a chronicle. To do this, however, is to render Camus a vast injustice. The epigraph he chose from Daniel Defoe's preface to *Journal of the Plague Years* states that "it is as reasonable to represent one kind of imprisonment by another, as it is to represent anything that really exists by that which exists not." This quotation invites the readers to transfer their attention from the literal to the figurative level of the novel and to see the intended richness and scope of the narrative.[2]

The Dominant Theme

One of the most rewarding methods of grasping the meaning of the novel is attained through an analysis of the major characters and their relationships to the plague. This approach is justified by a very simple and obvious interpretation of the all-encompassing symbol of plague. In the final section of the book, Dr. Rieux visits his old asthma patient. The distant clamor of the populace rejoicing in its newly-won freedom from the plague can be faintly heard in the bedroom. Dr. Rieux and the patient exchange a few introductory remarks, and then the old man says, "All those folks are saying: 'It was plague. We've had the plague here.' . . . But what does that mean—'plague'? Just life, no more than that" (277). Whether the novel is read as a symbolic treatment of the political problems of France at the time of the German occupation or of the metaphysical ones brought about by cosmic alienation in an absurd universe, the simple fact remains that Camus in the words of one of his most interesting and bizarre characters has equated plague with life. If the readers, in turn, accept this meaning of plague, then the entire novel becomes a statement about life and death or, more generally speaking, about the human condition in the twentieth-century Western world. It is at this point that the readers' thoughts evolve from a specific concern with the action, time, and place of the limited world of Oran in 194– into a general concern with the problems of life in all times.

Character Analysis

There is almost universal critical agreement that in general terms "the plague" as employed by Camus represents whatever threatens to prevent the fulfillment of human life within the given limits of an absurd world. Such a general interpretation is, however, unsatisfactory to most readers. They are left without any positive approach to the factual problems they have long been aware of. They still have no pattern or formula to follow and no hero to emulate. If, however, the readers turn from the external actions of the major characters to an analysis of the characters themselves, the pattern can be found. These major characters, ever aware of the complexity of their lives, are able to find meaning and happiness in an absurd world. It is especially the rather insignificant figure of Joseph Grand, the named hero of the book,[3] who embodies the central theme of the novel and can supply the readers' sought-after pattern.

According to the chronicle, Dr. Rieux considers Grand something of a mystery man. Tall and thin, he seems lost in his clothing, which he always chose a size too large under the illusion that it would wear longer. Though he has most of the teeth in his lower jaw, all the upper ones are gone. When he smiles his mouth looks like a small black hole in his face. Also he has the walk of a shy young priest, sliding along walls and slipping mouselike into doorways. And he exudes a faint odor of smoke and basement rooms. In short, he has the attributes of insignificance. It took an effort to picture him otherwise than bent over a desk. He evokes the feeling that he had been brought into the world for the sole purpose of performing the discreet but needful duties of a temporary assistant municipal clerk on the salary of sixty-two francs, thirty centimes a day.

Joseph Grand was not motivated by ambition. All he desired was a suitably comfortable life with enough leisure time for his hobbies. His salary was a mere pittance, but he did not draw attention to promises made to him in the past. The department head had been dead for some time, and Grand no longer remembered the exact terms of his employment. He could not easily express himself, and because of his inability to find the right words, he had performed his obscure ill-paid duties for the past twenty-two years. He felt a particular aversion against talking about his rights, and he hesitated to mention the department head's promises, for this would have implied that he was claiming his due and would have conveyed an audacity incompatible with the humble post he filled. On the other hand he refused to use expressions such as "your kindness," "gratitude," or even "solicit," which he thought belittled his personal dignity. He was one of those rare people who have the courage of their good feelings.

For quite some time Dr. Rieux knew only scattered facts about Grand's life. Grand's parents had died when he was very young, and his only surviving near relations were his sister and nephews whom he visited in France every other year. He talked about his special affection for the church bell in his town. Yet, to express such emotions caused him a great deal of effort, and this difficulty in finding his words had become the bane of his life. He brought up the subject of his difficulty each time he met Rieux, and it occurred to the doctor that perhaps Grand was trying to tell him that he was writing a book or something of the sort.

Grand finally unburdens himself to Rieux. For the first time since Rieux had known him, he becomes quite vocal. Though he still has trouble with his words, he nearly always succeeds in finding them. It was as if Grand had been thinking over for years what he now said. Grand tells Rieux about his love for and marriage to Jeanne. According to Grand they went on loving for a bit and then they worked and worked so hard that they forgot to love. Grand became so fatigued from hard work that he gradually lost grip of himself. He had less and less to say, and he failed to keep alive his wife's feeling that she was loved. Years of poverty and the gradual loss of hope in the future ruined their love. One day Jeanne left him to try to make a new start. Grand also had suffered but was unable to start afresh. He never stopped thinking about her, and he would have liked to write her a letter to justify himself. "But it's not easy," he tells Rieux. "I've been thinking it over for years. While we loved each other we didn't need words to make ourselves understood. But people don't love forever. A time came when I should have found the words to keep her with me—only I couldn't" (75–76).

After Paneloux's sermon something like a widespread panic begins in the town. Rieux and Grand are together and stop in a café for a drink. To the doctor's surprise Grand orders a small glass of straight liquor and drinks it all in one gulp. A moment later he suggests that they leave, and once out on the street Grand remarks that happily he has his work to divert his attention from the plague. Rieux asks him about his manuscript and the progress he is making. Grand explains that what he really wanted was that "on the day when the manuscript reaches the publisher, I want him to stand up—after he's read it through, of course—and say to his staff, 'Gentlemen, hats off!' " (94). Grand adds that the manuscript had to be flawless. He invites Rieux into his apartment to read him the opening sentence: "One fine morning in the month of May an elegant young horsewoman might have been seen riding a handsome sorrel mare along the flowery avenues of the Bois de Boulogne" (96). According to Grand, the sentence he read was only a rough draft. Once he succeeded in rendering perfectly the picture in his mind's eye, once his words had the exact tempo of this ride—the horse trotting, one-two-three, one-two-three—the rest would come more easily and, what was even more important, the illusion would be such that from the very first words it would be possible to say, "Hats off!"

The next we learn about Grand is that he is acting as a general secretary to the sanitary squads. He and Rieux had continued their frequent talks and Tarrou was often included in their meetings. Grand unburdened himself with increasingly apparent pleasure to his two companions, and they became interested and involved in his laborious literary task. Because he was constantly thinking about perfecting his sentence, he became absentminded in his work at the municipality. He was frequently excessively sentimental, and at such times he talked to Rieux about Jeanne. One evening shortly before Christmas, Rieux sees Grand with his tear-stained face glued to a shopwindow full of carved wooden toys. Rieux imagines a scene from long ago when Grand and Jeanne, happy in the love they felt for each other, stood before a shopwindow decorated for Christmas. And Rieux thought that "a loveless world is a dead world, and always there comes an hour when one is weary of prisons, of one's work, and of devotion to duty, and all one craves for is a loved face, the warmth and wonder of a loving heart" (237). As Rieux watches Grand, the old man collapses and has to be carried to the car.

Following his collapse, four events occur in rapid succession. Grand is diagnosed as a victim of the plague; Grand tells Rieux to burn his manuscript; Grand laments his inadequacy with words; and Grand's health rapidly improves. His sudden recovery is highlighted by the reappearance of the rats. The last reference to Grand in Rieux's journal reports that he had written to Jeanne and was feeling much happier. Also he had made a fresh start with his phrase. "I've cut out all the adjectives" (276), he said.

Briefly that is the story of the hero of *La Peste*. Camus places none of the intellectual burden of the human condition upon Grand. Grand in no way mentally suffers from the metaphysical anguish of Tarrou or even the frustrating torment of Rieux. He is less concerned with abstractions than he is with living. Yet he too has his "seemingly absurd ideal" and in his own way rebels against his bureaucratic, routine existence. Camus has chosen an average man as his hero, one who without knowing the philosophic language to express his thoughts is nonetheless an exemplification of our accidental and transitory presence on earth. Grand acts "as if" he knows. He does all the right things. When he is needed he is there to do whatever he can to alleviate the pain of his fellow citizens. He even sacrifices his most valued moments of work on his manuscript in order to devote more time and energy to the fight against the plague. He is consequently a superb illustration of Camus's statement in "Remarque sur la révolte" that the action of a trade union secretary who keeps his accounts up to date is "metaphysical revolt, just as much as the spectacular daring which sets Byron up against God!"[4] According to Camus true rebellion against injustice lies in the humble tasks of those who fight against it.

Grand's actions also emphasize the structure of the book. Throughout the novel's first section Grand's personality is gradually revealed, and he is described as an individual with his own cares and concerns. After the siege of plague is officially declared, Grand's individuality is emphasized less, and in the second part of the novel it is his involvement with the plague that is described. Grand's love for his wife specifically illustrates the suffering of separated lovers that is a major theme of part two. The third division is devoted to general rather than individual actions, and there is no mention of Grand. He appears again in the fourth section, and here his significance is underlined by his recovery from the plague. As might be anticipated, in this highly emotional portion of the novel, Grand is allowed the luxury of sentimentality. Grand's Christmas nostalgia is one of the most moving scenes of *La Peste*. In the final chapter of the narrative, Grand is ready to begin again. After burning sheets and sheets of manuscript, what he finds alive in his heart is his memory of Jeanne. He has written to her, has resumed his laborious writing task, and is again concerned with his personal needs. The one important distinction between Grand at the beginning of the plague and Grand after the plague has subsided is that he now has a greater degree of humanity than before. Through the process of the plague, he learned of his unity with others and is ready to make a fresh start of his life. This time he has "cut out all the adjectives." Even the uninitiated readers cannot fail to follow the progression of Camus's hero, and it is through the depiction of Grand's uncomplicated handling of the plague that Camus is able to combine philosophy and art and make his thoughts clear to a reading public not necessarily schooled in sophisticated philosophic thought.

It is Grand's actions that clarify the other characters' metaphysical struggle against the wretchedness and pain caused by the plague. In simply doing his job well, Grand is faithful to the idea of serving others without aspiring to the eternal or absolute, and in this way he is closely related to Dr. Rieux, the narrator of the action. Perhaps the least complicated figure in the book, Dr. Rieux fights the plague in the only way he knows. Trained as a physician devoted to the task of fighting illness and death, he views the plague as an acute manifestation of his constant enemy, death. He allows for no heroic interpretation of his actions. In his conversations with Tarrou and Father Paneloux, he again and again asserts that his commitment is only toward people's physical comfort and not toward their salvation. "Salvation's much too big a word for me," he tells Father Paneloux. "I don't aim so high. I'm concerned with man's health; and for me his health comes first" (197). Although he knows that any success he may have against the plague can only be provisional, he never regards this fact as a reason for abandoning the struggle against it. Rieux's revolt is earth centered without any appeal to a transcendental being. As he remarks to Tarrou, "Heroism and sanctity don't really appeal to me. . . . What interests me is being a man" (251). Rieux, unlike either Tarrou or Paneloux, comes to terms with the reality of the human condition, and he searches for no ideology that would allow him to escape it.

In many ways Rieux is Camus's spokesman. Like Camus he violently protests against the unintelligibility of a universe that permits the infliction of needless suffering; and again like Camus he feels an overwhelming compassion and respect for people and their pursuit of meaning. Rieux's total empathy with human needs is neither blind nor sentimental. He vehemently refuses "to love a scheme of things in which children are put to torture" (197). His attitude reflects Camus's comment to the Dominicans of Latour-Maubourg in 1949: "I share your horror of evil. But I do not share your optimism, and I continue to struggle against the universe in which children suffer and die."[5]

Camus's inability to accept orthodox theology is voiced in the novel by Rieux and is juxtaposed to the Christianity expounded by Father Paneloux. Paneloux's attitude toward the plague is in direct contrast to Rieux's. In his first of two sermons, Paneloux sees the plague as divine in origin and punitive in purpose. According to his theological principles, the human suffering brought about by the plague is willed by God and justified by the sins of the people of Oran. His militant form of Christianity demands that the true Christian accept the sacrifice and suffering of innocent men and women in the same way that he or she accepts the sacrifice of Christ. Both have been willed by God. The plague poses no religious conflict for the priest until he witnesses the death of M. Othon's child. He admits his revulsion at the sight of the child's agony, but he suggests that his feelings are caused by his inability to understand the final meaning of suffering and that "perhaps we should love what we cannot understand." (196). Paneloux's demand that we put aside our desire for rational explanations and accept God's will through faith is the subject of his second sermon. It differs from the earlier sermon in that he now uses the pronoun "we" rather than "you," and includes himself among those who have sinned. He no longer seeks a rationale for his belief that good finally results from evil, but he insists that this belief be accepted by faith. The only choice he offers is to "believe everything or deny everything." He asks for a total acceptance of God's will and a complete self-surrender of and disdain for the human personality. According to Paneloux, it is only in this way that we can make God's will our own. Paneloux's position recalls that of Heidegger, Jaspers, Shestov, Kierkegaard, and Husserl, which Camus had earlier rejected in *Le Mythe de Sisyphe*. Once faced with the absurdity of existence, none of these men remained true to it. All of them eventually destroyed it by deifying the contradiction between human need and the unreasonable silence of the world, and each of them took the unjustifiable leap into an irrational explanation that resolved the antinomy between human beings and the world.

Paneloux and Tarrou share the desire to discover values that will enable them to combat an imposed evil of nonhuman origin. Unlike either Rieux or Paneloux, however, Tarrou wishes to purge himself of all evil and transcend human limits. His intensely personal aim to become "a saint without God" (230), to attain a peace of mind with no feelings of guilt, is somewhat overshadowed by his more understandable desire to rid society of the plague. He identifies plague with the death penalty. In his confession to Rieux, Tarrou tells him of his childhood. As the son of a public prosecutor, he was first exposed to the horror of the death penalty at the age of seventeen when his father asked him to accompany him to court. Once in court he found that his attention was exclusively devoted to the condemned man. He could no longer think of this living being as a mere abstraction. The memory of the sandy-haired figure in the dock who looked like "a yellow owl scared blind by too much light" (224) changed Tarrou's entire life. Unable to bear life at home any longer, he became an agitator. In his mind the social order was based on the death sentence, and he felt that by fighting the established order he would fight against murder. In his struggle against society, however, he discovered a new form of plague. In witnessing an execution in Hungary, he experienced exactly the same dazed horror he had as a young man in his father's courtroom. And he realized that he had had the plague throughout all of the years in which he believed he was fighting it and that he had had "an indirect hand in the deaths of thousands of people" (227). This experience convinced him never to accept any argument that justified murder and never to consider "anything which, directly or indirectly, for good reasons or for bad, brings death to anyone or justifies others' putting him to death" (229). Tarrou realizes that he has not attained a state of complete innocence when he tells Rieux that "each of us has the plague within him" (229), and that he knows that in this world, our seemingly most insignificant actions may be responsible for the death of another.

Yet Tarrou strives to achieve the state of the innocent murderer by willfully joining forces with the victims and not the pestilences of the world.

With Tarrou plague takes on the specific meaning of the death penalty. It is an evil that ceaselessly afflicts everyone, and which the individual can struggle against, learn from, and survive, but not totally defeat. Tarrou's longed-for condition of absolute innocence remains an unattainable ideal, but his emotional reaction against capital punishment expresses Camus's protest in *La Peste* against a world where murder is legalized and human life is considered worthless. Tarrou shares Rieux's respect for individual life and in many ways underscores Grand's longing for understanding among all people when he says, "I'd come to realize that all our troubles spring from our failure to use plain, clean-cut language" (237).

The desire for simplicity and directness that Tarrou expresses and Grand finally realizes is an aspect of the book that is most openly exemplified by Madame Rieux, the doctor's mother. Because of her proximity to her son throughout the plague and her close relationship with Tarrou, she is frequently mentioned in the chronicle; yet she actually neither says nor does much of anything. It is through her felt presence that she creates a tranquil, serene mood that is difficult to describe. Tarrou stresses her "way of explaining things in the simplest possible words" (248). She voices none of the anguish of the male characters, and her ability to act intuitively without agonizing about her actions relates her to other feminine characters in Camus's works. Like Marie in *L'Etranger,* it is Madame Rieux who transmits an essential warmth and restfulness that cannot be conveyed by any of the other characters. Her gentle love and intuitive understanding are what the male characters long for in this time of pain and separation. The experience of separation is intently felt by each of the major characters and is one of the main themes of the novel. It is one of Camus's merits as an artist that this personal feeling is defined in only the most general terms. By limiting his description to a very vague mother image, Camus allows the readers to project their own feelings onto Grand's, Rieux's, and Rambert's desires for their loved ones.

It is Rambert who is willing to risk everything for the chance of personal happiness. During the period when the plague was gathering all of its force to lay waste to the people and the city of Oran, Rambert continued his monotonous struggle to recover his lost happiness and to prevent the plague from defeating him. From his experience in the

Spanish Civil War, he had learned that the only remedy against human anguish is found in the happiness that love brings, and he is determined to be reunited with the woman he loves. He tells Rieux that "Man *is* an idea, and a precious small idea, once he turns his back on love" (149). Although he eventually gives up his attempts to escape from Oran and willingly devotes his energies to fighting the plague, his actions stem from his inner conviction that individual happiness cannot exist in a plague-infested world. He has no belief in abstract ideologies. At the close of the book, Rambert is one of the happy few who welcome back their loved ones and for some time will be happy. He knew "that if there is one thing one can always yearn for and sometimes attain, it is human love" (271).

In contrast to Rambert's happiness, Cottard suffers every form of violence except death by the plague. Cottard is described as a man "who had an ignorant, that is to say lonely heart" (272), and he remains an ambiguous character throughout the book. He is a condemned man whose crime is never revealed. As the plague progresses and confines all the citizens of Oran, Cottard's anxiety diminishes, for the plague establishes a common bond between him and the others. In Oran all lives are threatened and no one is free to escape. It is the plague that allows Cottard a moment of reprieve and a taste of hope, which he desperately clings to until the city gates are reopened. At the end of the book, divested of all expectation and completely anxiety-ridden, he is led away by the police. Cottard, unlike the other characters, had not learned the value of human existence. He is introduced to the readers at the time of his attempted suicide, and he never seems to progress beyond his moment of despair. In *Le Mythe de Sisyphe,* Camus rejects suicide as an irrational evasion of the absurd. Human destiny, he says, with all its contradictions, must be accepted as it is and life must be lived in accordance with this acceptance. "Living an experience, a particular fate, is accepting it fully. Now, no one will live this fate, knowing it to be absurd, unless he does everything to keep before him that absurd brought to light by consciousness. Negating one of the terms of the opposition on which he lives amounts to escaping it. . . . Living is keeping the absurd alive. Keeping it alive is, above all, contemplating it . . . the absurd dies only when we turn away from it" (53–54). In this passage from *Le Mythe de Sisyphe,* Camus exalts the value of consciousness. This value is one of the most venerated ones in the humanist tradition, and in *La Peste,* Cottard embodies the negative side of that tradition by failing to keep the absurd alive and discovering the fragile hopes and joys that he shared with everyone.

The blend of Art and Thought

An analysis of the major characters of *La Peste* reveals that they embody the book's central theme and metaphysical implications. I do not wish to imply, however, that such an analysis captures the novel's total artistic and philosophic content. To consider the characters apart from their setting is to ignore an essential dimension of the novel. As the discussion of the major characters reveals—and there are fascinating minor ones—it is almost impossible to exhaust the significance of "the plague" by giving it a single interpretation. Its meaning is carefully woven into all aspects of the novel, combining as it does everyday elements with political and metaphysical ones into a powerful single image of plague. Camus equates the plague with different aspects of human misfortune. The specific manifestation of this misfortune is illustrated by the actions of a particular character or group of characters. For example, Grand's unhappiness is in part a result of the impersonal and mechanical aspects of much of modern life, and all of the characters, in one way or another, suffer from the loneliness caused by the lack of communication among people. Yet it is the collective fate of all the inhabitants of Oran, suffering and dying from the epidemic, that fuses these themes and provides the novel's focus. In "Remarque sur la révolte," Camus said, "In the absurd experience, suffering is individual. From the first movement of revolt, it is the adventure of all. . . . The malady which until then was suffered by one sole individual becomes collective plague" (1685). In *La Peste,* Camus expands the particular and temporal experiences of the people of Oran into a universal and timeless symbol of human suffering. By showing a progression away from private solutions of personal problems to a collective reaction to a common problem, he creates a symbol of universal significance and gives artistic form to his underlying philosophic thought.

One of the most striking examples of this blend of art and thought is contained in Camus's description of the feverish atmosphere that permeated the opera company's presentation of Gluck's *Orpheus.* In this episode art is a mirrored image of life. One could even draw an analogy between this scene and the play-within-a-play scene in Shakespeare's *Hamlet.* For just as in *Hamlet,* in which the action on the stage parallels the drama's overall action, here too the plight of Orpheus reflects the action within

La Peste. In act 1, Orpheus lamented his lost Eurydice and the audience applauded discreetly. In the second act, only a few people noticed that Orpheus introduced some tremolos not in the score and that he voiced an almost exaggerated emotion when begging the Lord of the Underworld to be moved by his tears. It was not until the duet between Orpheus and Eurydice in the third act that a flutter of surprise ran through the house as Orpheus "staggered grotesquely to the footlights, his arms and legs splayed out under the antique robe." The audience rose and began to leave the auditorium slowly and silently at first, but "gradually their movements quickened . . . and finally the crowd stampeded towards the exits . . . pouring out into the street . . . with shrill cries of dismay" (180). Without extending the episode's meaning beyond permissible limits, this scene can be interpreted as a specific illustration of the horror that permeates Oran in general in the same way that the individual anguish of Tarrou or Paneloux illustrates the metaphysical torment of humanity in general. It should also be noted that the structure of the scene from the initial point of the audience's indifference through their partial awareness to their complete recognition of the action being played out before them parallels the overall structure of the novel.

The incident at the theater is, along with the description of the Othon child's death, the episode with Grand at Christmas, and Tarrou's and Rieux's swim, among the novel's most significant scenes. These passages are emotional in content as well as in expression. As if signaling the reader their importance, Camus switches from the precise, almost detached, narration of the major portion of the chronicle to a highly poetical prose style that permits the reader to identify with the action. These poetic moments are infrequent, for a detachment from both the characters and their situations must be sustained so that readers can readily transfer their thoughts from the literal to the figurative and be attentive to symbolic inferences.

In the final analysis the effectiveness of *La Peste* can only be grasped through a direct reading. What we unquestionably learn is that as the plague bored its way into the lives of the people of Oran, oozed beneath locked doors and barred windows, crept into sterilized wards, and affected the rich, poor, happy, and wretched men and women, it did more than spread its horrible pestilence. As the plague became infectuous, each person had to forgo his or her individuality and unite forces with others. The cessation of the plague could not be a final victory, for the plague bacillus is never cured but runs its course only to return again. After the pestilence subsides most people return to their

former selves and once again hide the basic human core they had
revealed for such a brief moment. But amid the joyous celebration there
are a few who learn to omit the adjectives—a few who were better
people for having discovered that there is more to admire in people than
to despise. In the battle against the plague there is no victory; there is
only the awareness that, against all odds, we can resist, if not transform, the absurdity of the world.

Relationship of *La Peste* to Camus's Other Works

La Peste represents a reevaluation or extension of Camus's thought
but in no way negates the philosophy of his earlier writings. The world
remains the same absurd world of *Le Mythe de Sisyphe* and *L'Etranger,*
but here Camus investigates the possibility of finding a series of values
not only to satisfy his own demands but also to be commended to
others. He needed to know if it was possible to establish incontestable
values without the help of religion or of rationalist thought. This need
was acute for Camus, for at this time he was involved in a reevaluation
of his political engagement. At the end of World War II he discovered
that the ideas he had editorially expressed in *Combat* during the time of
the Resistance were only tenable in a limited way.[6] The war had forced
him to acknowledge that in an extreme situation one is justified in
denying the value of human life by destroying it; but having reached
this point in his thinking, after the end of the war he could not
continue to sanction any course of political activity that threatened to
destroy whole classes of people. He felt that the political creeds that
survived the war were in many cases based upon ideologies that unjusti-
fiably subordinated human life to abstract principles. In no way was
Camus prepared to continue an editorial fight for ideas that contra-
dicted his conviction that all human life is priceless in and of itself. He
resigned from the editorship of *Combat* in 1945 in order to complete *La
Peste,* and as late as 1949 he refused to return and take control of the
paper. This action does not so much reflect a change in Camus's original position as it does a disillusionment with the left-wing intellectuals
of postwar France. That he was no less concerned with the political and
social struggle than he was in 1938–39 or in 1944–45 is borne out by a
study of his next writings, the plays *L'Etat de siège* and *Les Justes.*

Chapter Six
The Theater of Revolt
The Intellectual and Political Scene

Until the end of 1947 Camus dealt impartially with the opposing political views of the East and the West. From 1948 on, however, he refused to conform to the ideas expounded by the intellectuals and neo-Marxists of the Parisian left-wing literati, and he openly identified himself with the democratic ideology of the West. It is at this time that the dichotomy between his literary and political activity, which had persisted throughout his earlier career, gave way to a desire to use literature to assert political influence. There is no doubt that to a certain degree *L'Etat de siège* (*State of Siege*), *Les Justes* (*The Just Assassins*), and the later *L'Homme révolté* (*The Rebel*) express Camus's reaction to the French intellectual and political scene of the 1940s and 1950s. Camus's arguments with François Mauriac, Sartre, and André Breton, along with his polemics against communism, are vividly reflected in his writing and in turn clarify many of the underlying moral and political problems considered in the literary works.

After the war Camus felt that the nihilism that brought the Nazis into power permeated the entire world. The actions of the United States and the Soviet Union demonstrated that the common threat of Hitler was not of sufficient duration to overcome the basic political mistrust and fundamental ideological differences between the two nations. The United Nations was little more than an idealistic debating society, and, in general, world leaders seemed to have learned very little from the war. Because of the bleak international situation, Camus found it necessary to abandon many of the hopes he had held for the postwar world, but he continued to believe in the world federation's goals of freedom and justice. Although he was aware that his role was not to transform the world, he persisted in his battle for what he considered the most vital moral issues of the day. Because he was again suffering from the aftereffects of tuberculosis, he took only a small part in the political events during the years 1948–51, but as *L'Etat de siège*,

Les Justes, and *L'Homme révolté* attest, he continued his search for the humanitarian spirit that could restore the value of an individual human life.

L'Etat de siège

Produced by Jean-Louis Barrault, against a background of striking music by Arthur Honegger and an imaginative décor by Balthus (Conte Balthazor Klossowiski de Rola), *L'Etat de siège* was first presented at the Théâtre Marigny on 27 October 1948. The cast was headed by Barrault as Diego, Maria Casarès as Victoria, Pierre Bertin as the Plague, Madeleine Renaud as his secretary, and Pierre Brasseur as Nada. Yet in spite of the magnificent visual and aural effects of the production and the imaginative methods employed by Camus in his use of the chorus and various dramatic styles, in Camus's own words, "When *L'Etat de siège* first opened in Paris, there was no dissenting voice among the critics. Truly, few plays have ever enjoyed such a unanimous slashing."[1] A work of art written by one of the world's leading authors has rarely received such disastrous critical reception.

The play's action involves the conflict between the regimentation imposed upon men and women by abstract ideologies and the freedom of the individual to enjoy the natural gifts of life. The plague, here represented by a human dictator, comes to the city of Cadiz in Spain. He is accompanied by his secretary, a woman who carries a notebook in which she has inscribed the names of the town's inhabitants. She can infect the citizens of Cadiz with the epidemic, or she can kill them at once by striking their names off the list. The Plague usurps the political power of the city and institutes a reign of terror by inaugurating laws that menace human values and reflect the worst features of a bureaucratic form of government. The Plague is assisted in his dictatorship by a drunken nihilist named Nada. A chorus of ordinary citizens hymns the beauties of nature, which the Plague and his cohorts deny them. The chorus also reflects the people's changing mood from confusion to anger to fear. Diego, a young man who attempts to alleviate the suffering of others, gradually emerges as the hero of the drama. He is in love with Victoria, the daughter of a judge; yet he is eventually forced to renounce his love so that Cadiz may be freed from the domination of totalitarianism and nihilism.

The fact that one of the central characters is named the Plague recalls Camus's novel, and indeed the opening scene of *L'Etat de siège* shares many similarities with the beginning of the novel. Before the Plague appears on stage, there is a pantomime in which an actor dies. A doctor arrives who first denies, and then admits, that the man died of the plague. Once the Plague makes his appearance, however, the similarities between the novel and the drama disappear. In the preface to the published version of the play, Camus says that although the subject is the same as that of *La Peste,* the play is not an adaptation of the novel. In the novel "plague" symbolized a force that can be struggled against and survived but never be defeated. In the play, however, the plague is specifically identified with a totalitarian force that can be fought and defeated. Unlike the novel, the drama emphasizes the eventual triumph over an evil created by totalitarian ideology. Camus says, "I did not seek to flatter anyone in writing *Le Etate de siège.* I wanted to attack directly a type of political society which has been organized or is being organized, to the right or to the left, on a totalitarian basis. No spectator can in good faith doubt that this play takes sides with the individual, in that which is noble in the flesh, in short, with terrestrial love, against the abstractions and the terrors of the totalitarian state, whether this be Russian, German, or Spanish."[2]

It is Camus's intention to create a modern drama that contains not only his analysis and criticism of twentieth-century society but also a possible solution to the problems he raises. At the close of the first of the play's three parts, the Plague clarifies the meaning of living in a state of siege. His speech expresses the negative aspect of totalitarian rule: "So take good notice, sentiment is banned, and so are other imbecilities, such as the fuss you make about your precious happiness, the maudlin look on lovers' faces, your selfish habit of contemplating landscapes, and the crime of irony. Instead of these I give you organiza-tion. That will worry you a bit to start with, but very soon you'll realize that good organization is better than cheap emotion."[3] In place of nonsensical ideas and righteous indignation, the Plague brings the people order, silence, and total justice. It is against these meaningless abstractions that Diego eventually revolts. In place of the "wild roses in the hedges, the signs in the sky, the smiles of summer, the great voice of the sea, the moments when man rises in his wrath and scatters all before him" (206), the Plague has sought to express everything in terms of figures and formulae, and to replace human values with a hypocriti-cal and contradictory interpretation of justice.

The conflict between Diego and the Plague outlines in dramatic form what is later expanded into Camus's philosophy of revolt. Not only does Diego oppose the abstract concepts of the Plague but he is also placed in a situation where he must choose between submission and revolt. He cannot appeal to traditional standards or supernatural sanction, for these mean nothing to him. Neither the church nor the law attempts to resist the Plague, and Diego feels himself alone and frightened. Until he overcomes the anguish and fear within himself, he cannot act. It is not until his confrontation with death that he realizes he is not alone and that many others are quite as much alone as he. "Each of us is alone because of the cowardice of the others. Yet though, like them, I am humiliated, trodden down, I'd have you know that you are nothing, and this vast authority of yours, darkening the sky, is no more than a passing shadow cast upon the earth, a shadow that will vanish in a twinkling before a great storm wind of revolt" (206). Through the discovery that he is not alone in his universe and that others share not only his fears but also his desires, Diego defines his revolt in the name of the more fragile joys of life, and he is willing to accept the consequences of his actions. He has thus acknowledged his total responsibility as a person, and completely independent of any metaphysical aid, he has fashioned his own destiny. Camus's criticism of the empty absolutes offered by the Plague in place of the rich beauties offered by the world, and his portrayal of a hero who, without any appeal to a supernatural authority, revolts against these absolutes, shows us the way we can triumph.

Relationship of *L'Etat de siège* to Camus's Other Works

As if to underscore the threat an empty society can inflict, normal human values are shown to be threatened not only by the excesses of dictatorships, but also by the hypocrisy of bourgeois morality. In many ways, Diego's situation in *L'Etat de siège* parallels that of Meursault in *L'Etranger*. Neither protagonist can derive any satisfaction from the outworn dictates of the church or the empty rulings of the law. Here Camus continues an underlying theme of both *L'Etranger* and *La Peste*. Meursault's actions were contrasted with the banal and empty actions of the bourgeois world, and like Diego, he found no solace from either the church or the law. In *La Peste* the same idea is repeated in Camus's satirical portrayal of Judge Othon's family and Father Paneloux's failure to find a reason for human suffering. These criticisms of dead and discredited values are again directly leveled in *L'Etat de siège*. When the priest tells the people of Cadiz that the plague "is the penalty with which God has ever visited cities that have grown corrupt; thus it is He punishes them for their mortal sin" (153), his words are almost an exact repetition of Paneloux's first sermon in *La Peste*. And there is little doubt that Judge Cassade in *L'Etat de siège* reflects the same hypocrisy of the law as that implied in *L'Etranger* and *La Peste*. All his life he based his decisions on an idea of absolute justice that failed to consider "the right of lovers not to be parted, the right of the criminal to be forgiven, the right of every penitent to recover his good name" (192). Through his portrayal of the priest and the judge, Camus convinces his audience that the morality expounded by formal clerical and secular laws contributes as much to the deadening atmosphere of the totalitarian state as does the autocratic power of the Plague himself.

Throughout the play the empty man-created world is contrasted to the natural splendors of the universe. This contrast recalls a dominant aspect of all of Camus's works. The world rich with "fresh fruit for the plucking, the poor man's cup of wine, a fire of vine twigs at which we can warm our hands" (213) is ever present to enjoy, and it negates not only the monotony of the totalitarian state but also renders Nada's nihilism impotent. His argument is senseless to those who enjoy nature's gifts: "if only one could suppress everything and everyone, wouldn't it be fine! Lovers . . . there's nothing I loathe more. . . . And children, filthy little brats! And flowers that goggle at you like half-wits, and rivers that have only one idea. So let's annihilate everything. . . . Long live nothing, for it's the only thing that exists" (178–79). In *L'Etat de siège*, Camus's rejection of nihilism repeats an earlier idea implicit in his letters to a German friend. Because there had been no ideology to oppose nazism, the Germans had discovered a reason for being in the abstractions of totalitarianism. Nihilism not only left the Germans alone and adrift, it also made them willing receptors for any abstraction that proffered a definition of life.

L'Etat de siège combines many of the ideas associated with Camus's thought. He himself said that *L'Etat de siège* "is, of all my writings, the one that most resembles me" (preface, viii). Unfortunately, as true as the statement may be, the drama's failure cannot be ignored. Camus attempted to profit from a direct exchange of ideas between himself and the audience; however, it is exactly on the level of communication that the play fails. No one denies the beauty and nobility of the ideas expressed, but the abstract handling of them produces indifference rather than involvement on the part of the audience. No matter how sympathetic we may be with Diego's trials, Diego himself is constantly dehumanized with words. Even the most anxiety-ridden of us finds it difficult to accept such verbosity as Diego's "O spirit of revolt, glory of the people, and vital protest against death, give these gagged men and women the power of your voice!" (209). The audience is exhausted rather than stimulated by this type of inward-gazing dialogue that in rhetorical fashion constantly questions the reasons for being. To believe in Camus's ideas, the audience must be able to accept the credibility of the characters who voice them. This is unfortunately impossible because of the unhappy combination of abstract ideas and highly stylized writing that characterizes *L'Etat de siège.*

Les Justes

Following the failure of *L'Etat de siège,* it is amazing that within the year Camus wrote what is generally considered to be his greatest dramatic achievement. Again preoccupied with the power of revolt over a particular kind of political and social folly, he openly criticizes the Stalinist methods employed by contemporary revolutionaries and contrasts their actions to those of the just assassins who in 1905 refused to ignore moral limits in their pursuit of a classless society. *Les Justes* was first performed in Paris at the Théâtre Hébertot in December 1950, with Serge Reggiani and Maria Casarés playing the roles of Kaliayev and Dora. In *Les Justes,* as in *Caligula,* Camus uses history as the basis for his plot. He borrows from the 1931 French translation of Boris Savinkov's *Souvenirs d'un terroriste (Memoirs of a Terrorist)* the factual account of the 1905 assassination of the Russian grand duke Serge, the czar's uncle. Savinkov describes how Kaliayev, a member of the group of idealistic terrorists, at first failed in his attempted murder because the grand duke was accompanied by his niece and nephew. It was not until later that he succeeded in throwing the bomb that killed the duke, and he was eventually executed by the state for his actions. Camus acknowledged his historical source not only in the program notes on sale in the theatre and in an article in the December 20th issue of *Combat,* but also in the preface to the American edition of the play. He wrote that the "events recounted in *Les Justes* are historical, even the surprising interview between the Grand Duchess and her husband's murderer. One must therefore judge merely the extent to which I manage to give plausibility to what was true."[4]

Inspired by the historical account of the revolutionary apostles of 1905, Camus borrowed heavily from Savinkov. Indeed, much of the dialogue of Kaliayev, Dora, and the grand duchess can be traced directly to this source; however, it would be unfair to consider the play as nothing more than a dramatization of a historical record. In the drama the past is not recreated for itself but for its current applicability. We are already aware of Camus's concerns with the political atmosphere of Paris at this time and his dread of the hypocritical aspects of many dogmatic pronouncements. *Les Justes* is in one respect an appeal to his contemporaries to reaffirm the integrity of the individual and to assume responsibility in the pursuit of justice. In an letter written to the magazine *Caliban,* he explains his point of view: "The 'modern' reasoning, as they say, consists in settling the problem: If you do not want to be executioners, you are choirboys, and vice versa. . . . Kaliayev, Dora Brillant, and their comrades refuted this base notion fifty years ago and told us that on the contrary, there is a dead justice and a living justice. Justice dies from the moment it becomes a comfort, when it ceases to be a burning reality, a demand upon oneself."[5]

The ultimate "demand upon oneself" that is made by Kaliayev is that he reject the momentary happiness and warmth of the world of human beings for the never-ending winter of the world of the just. This world is lonely, but it is the only one in which he can be a "doer of justice," and carry out his conviction that "when we kill, we're killing so as to build up a world in which there will be no more killing. We consent to being criminals so that at last the innocent, and only they, will inherit the earth" (245). The remarkable aspect of Kaliayev is that his motivation for murder is one of love rather than hate. Unlike the usual revolutionary, he bases his revolt upon a love for living rather than a belief in abstract principles. Before he leaves to assassinate the duke, he confesses to Dora that hatred is not a sufficient reason for murder and that he must go beyond hatred to love, to "sacrificing everything without expecting anything in return" (269).

Kaliayev's poetic idealism is contrasted to the harsh realism of Stepan. After Kaliayev had refused to throw the bomb because of the duke's niece and nephew, Stepan expresses the thought of the hardened revolutionary who is willing to sacrifice everything to accomplish the aims of the revolution. In answer to Kaliayev's insistence that even in times of revolution there are limits to human actions, Stepan protests that "there are no limits! . . . If you felt sure that, by dint of our struggles and sacrifices, some day . . . man will . . . look up toward the sky, a god in his own right . . . you would claim for yourselves the right to do anything and everything that might bring that great day nearer!" (258–59).

The contrast between Kaliayev's and Stepan's thoughts clarifies the difference between revolution and revolt. According to the revolutionary, his cause is just and must be fulfilled regardless of the consequences. He believes that all means that lead to the triumph of the cause are good. The rebel, on the other hand, is aware of the limits imposed upon his actions, and cannot act outside those limits. Kaliayev refuses to sacrifice the lives and happiness of those who are living today in return for the perfect happiness the revolution might achieve in the distant future. The insoluble paradox then arises between the good and the evil that are a part of the same act. It is necessary for Kaliayev to kill the grand duke in protest against the misery of the Russian people. The ideal is noble and just; the act, however, is criminal. By killing another individual, Kaliayev has overstepped the limits imposed by the natural order of things, and he has committed an unjust act in the name of justice. The only way that he can atone for his crime is through a willing consent to his own execution. He thus becomes his own judge and his own hangman. His death is his "supreme protest against a world of tears and blood" (294). Kaliayev's idea that assassins must pay for their crimes with their own lives is the only solution that Camus accepts as valid, and in his portrayal of Kaliayev, he artistically expresses a thesis he further explains in *L'Homme révolté:* "He who kills is guilty only if he consents to go on living or if, to remain alive, he betrays his comrades. To die, on the other hand, cancels out both the guilt and the crime itself."[6] For Camus, the 1905 Russian anarchists, who constantly questioned their right to murder and who willingly paid for each assassination with their own lives, illustrate the limit revolt can reach without betraying its initial ethical impulse.

In order to clarify the concepts of revolt and limits, Camus again contrasts the richness of the individual's ethical and moral code with the hollow tenets of state and church law. In the third act of the play, the dramatic center switches from Kaliayev's relationship with his fellow revolutionaries to his confrontation with the forces of social order and justice. In prison Kaliayev, like Meursault in *L'Etranger,* is questioned by representatives of orthodox law and religion. Skouratov, the chief of police, is not at all interested in Kaliayev's motives for his crime. What is essential for him is that Kaliayev admit his guilt and clear up the "slight untidiness" of the entire affair. According to his system of values, justice is only a matter of appearance. If Kaliayev atoned for his crime by informing the police about the other members of the organization, he would obtain the court's favor. Skouratov is deaf to any theoretical aspects of the murder. In answer to Kaliayev's statement that he threw a bomb against tyranny, Skouratov answers, "Perhaps. But it was a living human being whom it blew to bits" (282). The grand duchess also emphasizes Serge the man rather than Serge the incarnation of an idea. Through her we see the grand duke as a man who two hours before he died slept in an armchair "with his feet propped up on another chair" (287); a man who through love shared his wife's sorrows; a man who spoke of justice in "exactly the same voice" (286) as Kaliayev's. This man has been murdered by Kaliayev, and the grand duchess endeavors to convince him that it is his duty "to accept being a murderer" (288). According to the grand duchess, Kaliayev has only to acknowledge his crime for what it is and the road to God and salvation will be open for him. "God alone" can justify his act. Kaliayev, however, yearns not to meet God in a rendezvous on the steppes as in the Saint Dmitri legend but to come together with his fellow creatures on this earth. To capitulate and ask for grace would be to betray them and to isolate himself from them. His one strength derives from his sense of personal responsibility for his actions. By refusing to bargain either with the law or with God, he regains his peace of mind and chooses "death so as to prevent murder from triumphing in the world" (261).

With *Les Justes* Camus approaches his notion of modern tragedy more closely than in any of his other dramas. In this play the particular type of tension he insisted upon is easily demonstrable. Neither the duke, as a representative of the existent order, nor Kaliayev, as a representative of the just assassins, is completely right or completely wrong. Through the grand duchess we perceive an aspect of the grand duke that takes him out of the realm of abstraction and places him into the world of human beings. Although the ideology he supported was wrong, the duchess's love and admiration for him gives him a new dimension and at the same time makes his murder a more detestable act than it was before. On the other hand, although the beauty and sincerity of Kaliayev's ideal is never questioned, he sacrifices a great deal of his humanity in order to obtain this ideal. He is the first to recognize that he has overstepped the permissible limits when he chose to kill a human being for the sake of an ideal. Thus neither the rebel nor the object of his rebellion is either totally right or totally wrong, and the tension that results from the juxtaposition of these two forces creates a tragic mood of the highest order. This type of tension exists in all four of Camus's plays. Men and women are placed in situations against which they must revolt. In the two early dramas, they rebel agaist the irrational nature of fate; in *L'Etat de siège* and *Les Justes* it is a specified tyranny and injustice that are the objects of revolt. Yet, in all of the plays, in spite of the fact that our sympathies may center upon the rebellious, the forces that oppose them are also justifiable to a certain extent. At the moment of dramatic confrontation the fact that one force seems more just than another does not imply the inherent superiority of the one over the other. It is rather that at the particular chosen moment, the opposed force has gone beyond the acceptable limits.

Relationship of *Les Justes* to Camus's Other Works

Les Justes, like all four of Camus's dramas, reflects his philosophic concern with the doubts and aspirations of his own historical epoch. His plays are often difficult to understand within the context of his evolving metaphysical thought, but outside this context it is impossible to capture their full meaning. The difficulty lies not so much in the ideas as it does in the characters who convey them. One of Camus's greatest problems as a dramatist was his inability to portray convincing people while exploring metaphysical problems. His dramatic world is not only a world without God; it is often a world without men and women. In the least successful of his plays, the major characters amount to little more than abstract expressions of an idea. No one contests the nobility of the ideas they express, but it is difficult for the average theater-goer to empathize with a character who with inhuman singleness of purpose is totally committed to an idea. In his determination to combat the bourgeois complacency that he saw around him, Camus lectured to his audience on the higher ideals of love of earth, love between man and woman, and solidarity among all; and his lectures contain a directness of argument and a simplicity of plot that force the audience to recognize the importance of these values. But, once the nobility of the ideas is granted, the theater-goers are left with nothing to substitute for the stony happiness that they had before they were, so to speak, awakened from their lethargy. Despite the new force of revolt that he found, Camus never solved the problems of communication with ordinary people, of the place of tenderness in life, or of how to find happiness.

In none of Camus's dramas does the hero really establish contact with ordinary men and women. The people are never mentioned in *Le Malentendu;* in *Caligula* the Roman populace is only reflected in the lazy, cowardly actions of the patricians; in *L'Etat de siège* Diego saves the people of Cadiz but he never really communicates with them and he has to fight hard to refute the Plague's description of their cowardice and mediocrity; the revolutionaries in *Les Justes* love the Russian people but fear that this love will not be answered. Camus, the dramatist, faced much the same problem as that of his rebels. He was aware of the difficulty any playwright encounters if he or she attempts to convey philosophic concepts to an audience that wishes to be entertained rather than taught, and he never found the formula that allowed him to do both. Just as the clear consciousness of the rebels and the solutions found by them do little good if the gap between them and ordinary people is so great that the latter are unable to profit from this consciousness and these solutions, so too Camus's dramatic skills and noble views have little impact if they fall upon deaf ears. The positive aspect of the willing sacrifice that the rebel makes in order to carry out his or her revolt remains extremely remote to the average person. The rebel's cause is unquestionably good, but the fact that the struggle for this cause makes neither the rebel nor the world happier or better leaves the audience questioning the validity of the revolt.

For all of Camus's rebels—Jan, Caligula, Diego, Kaliayev—revolt seems to preclude ordinary happiness. They believe that the source of happiness is love between a man and a woman and that to turn away from such love leads to loneliness and isolation; yet they do not grant themselves the luxury of love. If their greater, or at least less selfish, love for humanity ended positively, their sacrifice would be understandable, but their deaths may or may not help humanity. The only assurance the plays give us is that the rebels' deaths bring suffering to the people who love them. None of the rebels either finds or brings happiness. Jan leaves the sunny country and Maria and dies alone and unrecognized; there is no certainty that Caligula's death will add to anyone's happiness; Diego is satisfied with what he has done but he is not happy; Kaliayev feels a sense of victory but not happiness. Theirs is a philosophic happiness that derives from having said no to those actions that exceed acceptable human limits.

Given the state of the universe that Camus presents, if one is to be faithful to revolt then there is no time to be young or happy. It seems possible though that this limited world is in part an accurate artistic reflection of life during and immediately following World War II. At this time Camus was optimistic about men and women, but perhaps overly pessimistic about society and about human action and interaction. With some justification Sartre accused him of loving individuals but not humanity. The world is not only a place in which people are killed for no reason, are homeless, and are strangers. Camus did not live long enough to shake off the influence of the war and to find a way to be happy. Besides, we have no way of knowing that he would have done so. Dora perhaps speaks for all the rebels when she says, "We are not of this world, we are the just." The insoluble conflict that is inherent in her cry separates the rebels from the rest of the world and makes the audience aware of a world that contains much good if much evil, and many joys if many sorrows.

Camus, too, must have felt this need for a positive action that would bring a positive result. In his next major writing, *L'Homme révolté,* he searches for moral values in a world where the death of God has been proclaimed. In much the same way that Dostoevski proves through Christianity that values do exist, Camus sets out to prove that revolt in its true meaning is the only recourse in a world void of religious faith. Following the ideas latent in the four dramas, Camus illustrates that revolt protests against the suffering and injustice of an absurd world and in itself creates a moral value based on the idea of moderation. He employs the solution to the problem of necessary political murder, demonstrated by the just assassins in *Les Justes,* in order to illustrate the limits revolt must assert if it is to be faithful to its original moral impulse. Revolt now becomes specifically defined as the impulse that drives us to defend human dignity.

Chapter Seven
The Rebel
The Philosophical Problems

In 1943 Camus argued in *Le Mythe de Sisyphe* that the certainty of death made life itself a charade and therefore absurd. He compared our fate to that of the Greek mythical figure of Sisyphus who was eternally condemned by the gods to roll a huge boulder up to the top of a hill, only to see it roll back down again. But from Sisyphus's seemingly futile and certainly never ending task, Camus drew a particular kind of strength. Rather than surrender to a world without hope and meaning, he insisted that life and work must go on. Indeed, it is from the recognition and acknowledgment of the crushing truth of our absurd fate that we win our strange victory over the limits imposed upon us by nature. Through his reflections on the absurd, Camus could say in 1943 that the only serious philosophic problem was suicide; but confronted with totalitarianism, the occupation, the Resistance, liberation, the communist successes in France, and the events of the cold war, he soon discovered that the stoic comfort offered by Sisyphus was of little solace or value. As early as 1943 and 1944, although still enmeshed in the theory of the absurd, Camus began in his *Lettres à un ami allemand* a search for some way to transcend the nihilism of his early writings; and in 1945 with the publication of the essay "Remarque sur la révolte" he moved closer to the idea of revolt as it is imaginatively presented in *La Peste* and logically argued and documented in *L'Homme révolté (The Rebel)*. By 1951, the publication date of *L'Homme révolté*, Camus's thought had undergone notable changes. Because of the inadequacy of the absurdist ethic, he undertook a reexamination of his earlier conclusions. Without negating the premise of *Le Mythe de Sisyphus*, he endeavored to find some satisfying answer to the absurdity, suffering, and injustice that men and women must endure.

The Purpose

The general purpose of *L'Homme révolté* is stated in the introduction to the book. Just as *Le Mythe de Sisyphe* opens with a meditation upon the problem of "judging whether or not life is or is not worth living"; so this work begins with a meditation upon the problem of "finding out whether innocence, the moment it becomes involved in action, can avoid committing murder" (4). To find an answer to this question Camus proposes to follow "into the realm of murder and revolt, a mode of thinking that began with suicide and the idea of the absurd" (5).

Reappraisal of the Absurd

The idea of the absurd is essentially the same as in *Le Mythe de Sisyphe,* but in his reappraisal of it, Camus seeks to discover a mode of action that will teach us how to live in the world as it is. He does not dismiss the absurdist attitude, but he now sees the absurd as a limited perception among many possible views. He recognizes it as a legitimate sensibility that takes into account the universal malady of despair that existed between the wars, but one that does not provide the values to judge human actions, to progress beyond nihilism, and to create moral order. The reader, then, is first referred to a new analysis of the argumentation presented in *Le Mythe de Sisyphe.* According to Camus, the sense of the absurd, when one first undertakes to deduce a rule of action from it, makes murder seem a matter of indifference. If one believes in nothing and if nothing has value, it naturally follows that nothing is important and everything is permissible. Since nothing is true or false, good or bad, we should be willing to kill in order to gain the most powerful and most effective position for ourselves. As a matter of fact, the logic of this argument does not hold up under close analysis; for the absurdist doctrine, after having shown that killing is a matter of indifference, actually condemns killing in its most important deduction. Camus reminds the reader that the final conclusion of the absurdist process is the rejection of suicide and the insistence upon a persistent encounter between the universe and human beings. It is clear that through the rejection of suicide and the consequent recognition of human life as the single good, the absurdist analysis cannot logically defend murder. "Absurdist reasoning cannot defend the continued existence of its spokesman and, simultaneously, accept the sacrifice of others' lives" (7). Thus the same notion that permitted the absurdist to think that murder was a matter of indifference here undermines its justification.

As soon as the absurd is understood to require one to continue living, it becomes contradictory. The very act of living necessitates choice and judgment, but choice and judgment cannot be exercised in an absurd world. The absurd, then, considered as a rule of life, is contradictory and unsatisfactory. It is also incompatible with discussions of its own nature. Simply by being expressed, it gives a minimum of coherence to incoherence and introduces consequence where, according to its own tenets, there is none. "The only coherent attitude based on non-signification would be silence—if silence, in its turn, were not significant" (8).

Faced with the insoluble contradiction raised by absurdist reasoning, Camus discovers in this dilemma a new area for investigation. Although it is true that absurdism leads up a blind alley, it can open a new field of investigation by returning upon itself. The recognition of the absurd automatically implies the existence of some other value by which to judge it absurd. To have negated one value implies the acceptance of some other value. The absurd, then, is a movement of revolt that is affirmation as well as negation. And it is the affirmative aspect of the absurd that interests Camus at this time. In people's refusal to be what they are, in their insistence upon "order in the midst of chaos and unity in the very heart of the ephemeral" (10), Camus sees some home for legitimate action that will end useless murder and allow us to act in accord with individual human worth and potentiality. But before we can learn how to act—indeed, whether to act—the attitudes, pretensions, and conquests of rebellion must be investigated; and it is to this problem that the major portion of the book is directed.

The Three Consequences of Revolt

In the first section of the essay proper, Camus seeks to define "rebel" and "revolt." Using a thought process similar to that employed in the past, Camus employs an individual experience to clarify rather abstract terminology. In order to ascertain the significance of revolt, he begins by analyzing the relationship between a master and his slave at the precise moment when the slave decides that he cannot obey some new command issued by his master. And his refusal, according to Camus, has a double implication. The slave, of course, rejects the force that oppressed him in the past, but perhaps more significantly, he insists upon his right not to be oppressed beyond a tolerable limit. Existentially it can be said that revolt represents the real moment of birth for the individual, for it is through his refusal to obey that the slave realizes his own value. He is independent and free. Up to this time he was acted upon, but through his revolt he demands respect for himself, identifies himself, and becomes a member of the community of free people. The first consequence of revolt, then, is to make individuals aware of their worth as human beings and of their potentiality as members of the human race.

As the meaning of revolt becomes clarified, the slave arrives at a point where he refuses oppression for any reason and declares himself ready to die in defense of his rights as an individual. "What was at first the man's obstinate resistance now becomes the whole man, who is identified with and summed up in this resistance" (14–15). The slave proclaims the part of himself that he wishes to be respected as preferable to everything, even to life itself. Up to this time he had accepted orders and compromise; but from the moment of rebellion, a new awareness is born, an awareness of a universal good or value that everyone, including the oppressor, possesses. The slave becomes so convinced of his human right that he is ready to accept death and die as a consequence of his rebellion. And it is through this fact that he demonstrates his willingness to sacrifice himself for the sake of a common good that he considers more important than his own destiny. If he prefers the risk of death to the negation of the rights he defends, it is because he considers those rights more important than himself. Therefore he acts in the name of certain values that are still indeterminate, but which he feels are common to himself and to everyone else. According to Camus, the analysis of rebellion has led "at least to the suspicion" that a human nature does exist. "It is for the sake of everyone in the world that the slave asserts himself when he comes to the conclusion that a command has infringed on something in him which does not belong to him alone, but which is common ground where all men . . . have a natural community" (16). It is the recognition of a universal human nature that is the second consequence of the slave's revolt.

The third consequence of revolt is closely linked to and follows quite naturally from the second. Camus concludes that the discovery of a universal human nature leads to the fact of human solidarity. When the slave revolts, he demands respect for himself but only insofar as he identifies with a natural community. His rebellion is always linked with his awareness of the solidarity of the individual with the human race, and he cannot act selfishly, for he alone is only a minute part of the values he wishes to defend. He needs to identify himself with others and reveal that part of himself that is worth defending. "I revolt, therefore we are" is the formula Camus uses to summarize this concept.

In revolt, then, the slave, and ultimately everyone, becomes conscious of what he is and what the world is, and he realizes his solidarity with the human race. He is still within an absurd universe, but he has learned that through revolt he can create his own values and proceed beyond the anguish of resignation and silence. Camus's intention is obviously moral in nature, for the type of revolt that he has in mind has little underlying self-interest and seeks to progress to a valid ethical ideal based upon the idea of moderation.

The Limit in Space and Time

At this stage in the argument, Camus has defined and generalized the problem of revolt. He now proceeds to limit his discussion in both space and in time. For seemingly logical reasons, he confines his examination of the manifold manifestations of revolt to the Western world during the past two centuries. He justifies his choice first by stating that the spirit of rebellion finds little means of expression either in societies where inequalities are great or in those where there is absolute equality. According to Camus, "The spirit of rebellion can exist only in a society where a theoretical equality conceals great factual inequality" (20). It is Western society with its seeming equality and actual inequality that provides the best stage for rebellion. His reasons for limiting the major portion of his investigation to the time following the French Revolution are equally sound. Camus sees 1789 as the starting point of modern times, because the people of that period wished to overthrow the principle of divine right and to introduce to the historical scene the forces of negation and rebellion that had become the essence of intellectual discussion in the previous centuries. The murder of King Louis XVI symbolizes the secularization of Western history and the dematerialization of the Christian God. Up to this time God played a part in history through the medium of the kings; but when His representative in history is killed, there is nothing but a semblance of God, relegated to the heaven of principles. With the death of God's representative on earth men and women became free to attempt to discover a new illumination and a new happiness. It was from this historical moment forward that people were free to rebel, free from a society whose problems were resolved by an appeal to a God who created and was responsible for everything. Henceforth the individual had to formulate morality in reasonable terms and search for rules of conduct "outside the realm of religion and its absolute values" (21).

Religion and Revolt

Although orthodox religious concepts are eventually negated in Camus's search, a strong moral intention underlies his concept of revolt; this becomes apparent in his discussion of the relationship between religion and revolt. According to Camus, rebels defy more than they deny. Originally they do not suppress God. They protest against the human condition both for its incompleteness because of death and its wastefulness because of evil; and in their rejection of their mortality, they refuse to recognize God or the power that compels them to live in this condition. The metaphysical rebels are therefore not so much atheists as blasphemers, for their protest can only have meaning if they first posit an omnipotent God; and their revolt does not become atheistic until they subject God to human judgment and deprive Him of His power. In their demand for equality with God, the rebels usurp the power once granted to God and alone assume the responsibility for the creation of justice, order, and unity, which they formerly sought in vain. They then begin to mold the dominion of men and women. If they remain faithful to their original purpose and do not abandon themselves to complete negation or total submission, their revolt will be positive. It is their failure to remain true to the positive aspects of their revolt that eventually leads them to betray the moral value implicit in their revolt and to choose the comfort of tyranny or slavery.

History of Revolt

At this point in the essay, Camus begins to describe the history of revolt in the Western world. It is perhaps more accurate to say that he discusses the perversions of revolt. First, there is the metaphysical nihilism that demands of God absolute freedom for the individual and defeats itself in a mystifying dandyism; second, the abstract declaration of democratic values that produced the revolutionary tyranny of 1793; third, the Hegelianism that identifies rebellion with history and enslaves men and women in dialectic; fourth, the irrational terrorism of fascism; and finally, the rational terrorism of Stalinism. Thus Camus pursues the history of a tradition of rebellion ultimately destroyed by a dehumanizing revolution. In the final section of the essay, disillusioned by the long, murderous, and deceptive history, Camus returns to the humanistic ideals of the Renaissance and rediscovers justness and proportion in the Mediterranean culture of Spain, Italy, Greece, and North

Africa. Thus the total movement of the essay proceeds to the final exposure of the paradox whereby revolt in the name of freedom and justice flounders and collapses if it is not directed toward a system of ethics that can serve a world beyond nihilism.

Metaphysical Rebellion

It would be tedious and unnecessary to paraphrase Camus's comments on the history of revolt from the marquis de Sade onward; however, it is necessary to elucidate some of his major thoughts in order to follow the movement of his discussion. In the section of the book devoted to metaphysical rebellion, he argues that during the past 150 years, the same human protest has been repeated over and over again. From Sade onward, all metaphysical rebels, regardless of their different guises, affirmed the solitude of human beings and the absence of any kind of morality. But once having denied the existence of God, they then set about to reconstruct creation according to their own concepts and consequently to usurp the power that traditionally was God's. Although Sade's and the romantics' original intent was in accord with the nature of rebellion, the rebels of the past have ultimately been unfaithful to the true nature of revolt. According to Camus, the rebel must seek a moral philosophy or religion that demands unity in the world even if the world denies that life has any meaning. As soon as the rebels lay aside this demand and abandon the tension that it implies either for the world of appearances or for murder and destruction, they have rejected the burden of rebellion and destroyed the noble end they initially sought.

Dostoevski and Nietzsche

It is the logical revolt of Dostoevski and Nietzsche that is the most appealing to Camus. These two men denied God in the hope of achieving a more profound existence for men and women. Unlike the romantics who sought to raise themselves to the level of God, Dostoevski places God on trial, ultimately rejects Him, and attempts to replace the reign of grace with the reign of justice. He does not endeavor to reform anything in creation, but rather sets out to claim the right to free himself from all moral bonds and to reject all law other than his own. Nietzsche proceeds a step further. He rids the world of God and of moral values and leaves human beings alone and without a master. The logic of Dostoevski's character Ivan Karamazov, "if nothing is true, everything is permitted," is replaced by the profounder statement by Nietzsche, "if nothing is true, nothing is permitted." Nietzsche thus avoids Ivan Karamazov's ethical dilemma, but he in turn subjects men and women to the heartbreaking task of accepting everything. Both Dostoevski and Nietzsche sought a reign of justice in logical rather than moral revolt, but their unwillingness to go beyond nihilism doomed their revolt to a passive acceptance of the world as it is and to ultimate failure. Since both Dostoevski and Nietzsche affirm the sovereignty of the individual, no one's actions can be judged as criminal or sinful. The individual is again alone and revolt has led only to a desert of solitude in which the solidarity of all can never exist.

Camus views the revolt of the nineteenth century as primarily individualistic in nature and negative in its results. Since it failed to escape from nihilism, it inevitably led to a kind of anarchy that was easily perverted to justify detrimental action. Thus the revolt of Dostoevski led to the justification of revolution just as surely as Nietzsche's ideas became the foundation of nazism. The fact that Dostoevski's and Nietzsche's ideas were misunderstood by the revolutionaries and the National Socialists in no way lessens the lethal effect that these ideas perpetuated. In their demand for what Camus calls the intemperance of absolutism—their desire for the absolute in philosophy—these men betrayed the initial concept of revolt and relegated the integrity of the individual to second place. In the teachings of true revolt, no one can demand for oneself more liberty than is consistent with the liberty of his or her neighbor. Rebels such as the comte de Lautréamont and Arthur Rimbaud were equally guilty of absolutism. Initially these poets expressed the idea of revolt purely, but as soon as they wearied of the effort demanded by their revolt, they almost automatically ended in banal conformism. The early poetry of Lautréamont and Rimbaud lies in direct contrast to their later work or lives. *Les Chants de Maldoror* and Rimbaud's poetry are pure expressions of revolt, but *Les Poésies* and Rimbaud's later life clearly indicate both poets' failure to sustain the effort demanded by absolute revolt. The ideas expressed in *Les Poésies* and Rimbaud's letters from Harrar illustrate the poets' absolute conformity to banality.

Twentieth-Century Rebellion

In the twentieth century the individualistic revolt of the nineteenth century degenerates into a combination of subjective anarchy and the objective principles of Marxism. The surrealists whom Camus cites as his witnesses are as guilty as Lautréamont and Rimbaud of stifling their revolt in dismal conformity. Absolute rebellion, total insubordination, and the humor and cult of the absurd were the terms the surrealists employed to define their primary intent; but unable to reach the goals of their movement, they sought to reconcile their subjective aims with Marxism. Because of two basic contradictions in principles, the combination had to fail. In the first place, in its insistence upon the submission of the irrational, Marxist theory directly opposed the surrealists' defense of irrationality; and second, while Marxism tended toward conquest, surrealism tended toward unity. The surrealists sought to reconcile Marx's "let us transform the world" with Rimbaud's "let us change life"; but since the first leads to the conquest of the world and the second to the unity of life, the desired reconciliation remained an impossible dream.

According to Camus, neither the individualistic rebellion of the nineteenth century nor the subjective anarchy of the twentieth century has retained the tension necessary to true rebellion. He sees the blind acceptance of reality is just as destructive to rebellion as its total rejection. In either case the intended rebellion assumed only one of the terms of the perpetual tension that must exist if rebellion is to be faithful to itself. While the tension remained, moral value could exist, but once the tension was eliminated, only death, violence, and moral nihilism remained. The only true rebellion open to us must retain its moral intention, for from the moment we decide to exclude ourselves from grace and to live by our own means, the only kingdom open is the kingdom of justice. This kingdom, for Camus, cannot be won by political conquest; for if metaphysical rebellion joins forces with revolutionary movements, the rebels abandon their original desire for the control of their own existence and set out in search of world conquest by way of an infinitely multiplied series of murders.

Revolt in History

It is to the investigation of revolt in history that Camus now turns his attention. Just as the history of metaphysical rebellion began with Sade, Camus sees the time of historical rebellion as beginning with Sade's contemporaries, the regicides, "who attack the incarnation of divinity without yet daring to destroy the principle of eternity" (108). But before beginning his discussion of the history of revolution, Camus draws a careful distinction between his understanding of the words *rebellion* and *revolution*. Rebellion, to him, is no more than an incoherent pronouncement that leads into the realm of ideas, whereas revolution originates in the realm of ideas and seeks to inject these ideas into historical experience. In his words, "While even the collective history of a movement of rebellion is always that of a fruitless struggle with facts, of an obscure protest which involves neither methods nor reason, a revolution is an attempt to shape action into ideas, to fit the world into a theoretic frame" (106). Although revolution may be initiated by revolt, because of its effort to establish a new social order at the expense of the existing order, it inevitably introduces the idea that expediency is a sufficient justification for any and all action. Once murder, conquest, and enslavement are legitimatized, the original cause of revolt "to affirm the dignity of man in defiance of things that deny its existence" (105) gives way to ideological absolutism, and the rights of each individual to a measure of human happiness have been sacrificed to a vague promise of some future, perfect social order.

Hegel

It is with the German philosopher Hegel, then, that the idea of God is finally destroyed. The principles of justice, reason, and truth, which were consecrated by the French Revolution are now relegated to the end of history and can be attained only when the historical process is completed. According to Hegel, there are no values other than those sanctioned by the historical process. The reasonable absolutes that were recognized by Jean-Jacques Rousseau and Louis Antoine Léon de Saint-Just as guides for action, now become goals in themselves that must be achieved by action. To Camus the historical Absolute that Hegel postulates in place of God is a further dehumanization of the idea of revolution; for if men and women have no control over their destiny and are only a part of the inevitable historical process, their individual actions cannot definitively be judged as either right or wrong. In addition, if history is the only judge of action, it necessarily follows that the conqueror is always right and the defeated is always wrong, for it is only the conqueror who can move on with the flow of history. Moral values as such must then constantly shift and be adapted to the historical times. If an individual seeks to express values other than those sanctioned by the historical moment, his or her murder can always be justified in the name of some eventual good. Under this system the rights of the individual must be sacrificed to the state, and those who hinder the realization of the state must be killed.

It is not surprising that Camus concludes that all forms of totalitarianism derive their justification from Hegel. According to his reasoning in *L'Homme révolté,* radical Hegelianism has perfected the philosophy of efficacity and has transformed the history of revolt by calling people into action to bring about the final realization of their human nature. This placement of the fulfillment of real human nature at the end of the historical process is in complete disagreement with the philosophy of revolt. It will be remembered that one of the first consequences of the slave's rebellion was his recognition of his solidarity with the human race. If, as in Hegelianism, the recognition is postponed to an indefinite future time, then men and women become slaves of the future and are eventually ignored, repressed, disciplined, and even murdered for the greater good of the state. In the historical process, the present is only important as a step to the future, and people are used as a means to an end. This idea is in direct opposition to Camus's constant insistence in all of his major writings that men and women must be regarded as ends in themselves. According to Camus, the consequences of radical Hegelian thought are reflected in the rational and irrational state terrorism of the twentieth century, but for the moment he pauses in the midst of his discussion of the general movement of revolutionary thought to recount the story of the *meurtriers délicats* (scrupulous assassins) as the unique example of fidelity to the values of revolt.

Les Meurtriers délicats

Camus insists that the 1905 Russian terrorists, whom he calls the *meurtriers délicats,* marked the highest peak of revolutionary momentum. By assassinating the grand duke Serge, this small group of young men and women hoped to recreate a community founded on love and justice. In this respect they were no different from the hundreds of other dedicated men and women who preceded them in time and who also sought to create new values through attempted assassinations. The factor that distinguishes this particular group from all others is that they, tortured by contradictions, gave birth to a value that henceforth opposed tyranny and helped authentic liberation. In their ability to combine in themselves a respect for human life in general and a contempt for their own lives, and in their recognition of the inevitability of violence and their own inability to justify it, they lived the tensions and paradoxes that Camus finds necessary to revolt. Because they were able to keep the terms of both the paradoxes alive and were willing to pay for their guilt with their own lives, they were able to preserve the true character of revolt in a way that later revolutions were unable to sustain. As seen in Camus's drama *Les Justes,* the 1905 Russian anarchists, who constantly questioned their right to murder and who willingly paid for each assassination with their lives, illustrate the limit revolt can reach without betraying its initial ethical impulse.

The 1905 terrorists' triumph over nihilism was, however, extremely short-lived. Their individual terrorism, which successfully proclaimed human dignity, soon gave way to the well-known horrors of state terrorism. In the nazi and fascist regimes, which claimed to be based upon the philosophies of Nietzsche and Hegel (Hitler makes use of Nietzsche; Mussolini of Hegel), the rights of the individual were usurped, and the historical situation rather than the individual became the arbiter or moral values. In both Hitler's and Mussolini's attempts to construct empires based on state terrorism, the dictators emphasized the irrational. They were the first to construct a state on the concept that "everything is meaningless and that history is only written in terms of the hazards of force" (178). According to Camus, the reason their hopes to dominate the world failed is implicit in the underlying tenets of their philosophies. They never really had any pretensions to a universal empire, even though they aimed at the eventual domination of the world. "At the very most, Hitler . . . was diverted from the provincial origins of his movement toward the indefinite dream of an empire of the Germans that had nothing to do with the universal City" (186). On the contrary, the dream of world unification is to Camus the aspiration of Russian communism and not that of fascism. "Russian Communism . . . has appropriated the metaphysical ambition that this book describes, the erection, after the death of God, of a city of man finally deified" (186).

Karl Marx

In the next section of *L'Homme révolté,* Camus exerts considerable effort to clarify the ideological basis of Russian communism. In the English translation of his work, almost sixty pages are devoted to the criticism of the state terrorism that resulted from the teachings of Karl Marx. This fact alone accounts for the tremendous success the book enjoyed among right-wing intellectuals in France and abroad; but as was true in his criticism of Nietzsche and Hegel, here too Camus distinguishes between Marxist theories and the interpretation or manifestation of these theories in fact. He points out that the Marxists who have made history have extracted the prophetic and apocalyptic aspects of Marx's doctrine without remaining faithful to the method Marx outlined in his writings. But, again as in the case of Nietzsche and Hegel, Camus sees inherent contradictions and inconsistencies in Marx's basic doctrine; and it is to the discussion of these contradictions that he devotes most of his energies.

Although Marx claims that his theories are based on pure reason, Camus finds them to be no more founded on reason than is any other prophetic faith. He sees Marx's method as a mixture of determinism and prophecy that has a great deal in common with Christianity and bourgeois culture. Like Christianity, Marxism superimposes an ideological structure on the world. And like bourgeois culture, Marxism reflects an optimistic belief in technical and scientific progress that will eventually aid men and women in their attempt to conquer nature. Unlike Christianity, Marxism replaces God and all transcendent principles with a belief in a future utopia; and in its relegation of values to the future, it loses its scientific foundation and becomes no more or no less than any other supposition.

Camus also sees a contradiction within Marx's untenable belief in the dialectical concept of history. He argues that complete acceptance of the dialectical principle negates the end of history to which the Marxist revolution directs itself. Since the Marxist dialectic is only pure movement, which seeks to negate all that is other than itself, it cannot imply an end to something that by admission has no beginning. The very nature, then, of the dialectic refutes Marx's belief that the class struggle would eventually be replaced by a classless society; for by necessity, once the classless society was attained, a new undefined antagonism would have to come into being.

These discrepancies in Marx's theory, coupled with his failure to foresee the development of society as it actually occurred, led to an eventual reinterpretation and bastardization of his system by the Russian Communists. What Camus deplores the most in contemporary Marxism is its failure to remain faithful to the original spirit of revolt. Ignoring its initial insistence upon human innocence, revolt, in the hands of the Russian Communists, denies the existence of a human nature and ignores every moral precept. Methods of thought that originally claimed an intent to realize the total individual have disintegrated into an acceptance of the logic of history and the mutilation and destruction of all.

To the slave's "I rebel, therefore we exist" metaphysical rebellion added, "We are alone," and attempted to construct existence with appearances. Now, absolute revolution has carried the original statement even further by supposing the malleability of human nature and its possible reduction to the conditions of a historical force. According to Camus, revolution has betrayed rebellion in two ways. First, in its attempt to establish a perfect social order, the world of power is constantly at odds with the less than perfect human nature that rebellion affirms. Second, revolution, in its rush to attain its longed for social order, justifies the murder of those who detain its progress, and in this way it surpasses the limits that rebellion sets for itself. Furthermore, through its affirmation of "a limit, a dignity, and a beauty common to all men" (251), rebellion demands extending this value to everything and everyone. "The former starts from a negative supported by an affirmative, the latter from absolute negation and is condemned to every aspect of slavery in order to fabricate an affirmative that is dismissed until the end of time. . . . The first is dedicated to creation so as to exist more and more completely; the second is forced to produce results in order to negate more and more completely" (251). Rebellion says that revolution must try to act, not in order to come into existence at some future date, but in terms of the obscure existence that is already made manifest in the act of insurrection. To the "I rebel, therefore we exist" and the "We are alone" of metaphysical rebellion, rebellion at grips with history adds that "instead of killing and dying in order to produce the being that we are not, we have to live and let live in order to create what we are" (252). Since this rule is neither formal nor subject to history, Camus feels that it can best be described by examining it in its pure state of artistic creation.

Artistic Creation and Revolt

In the next section of L'Homme Révolté, Camus discusses the relationship between artistic creation and revolt. He correlates our desire for unity and beauty expressed in art with our desire for order expressed in political institutions, and he affirms the ability of art to correct material disorder and to give us our longed-for refuge from the passage of time. The major points of Camus's aesthetic theories are discussed in Chapter Nine of this book; however, it should be pointed out here that this part of *L'Homme révolté* serves as an excellent bridge between the narration of the history of revolt and the poetic presentation of revolt recommended in the final chapter of the essay.

The Dilemma

After the investigation of error, treason, and darkness that constitutes the major sections of the essay, Camus appears to recognize that rebellion is caught in an irreconcilable dilemma. Although the rebels have a clear concept of justice, as soon as they act, they find themselves committing injustice. After metaphysical revolt destroyed the concept of God, the revolutionary expression of revolt ended in the murder of men and women. But murder cannot be reconciled with revolt. By definition revolt affirms the liberty of all in the face of a common destiny, whereas murder contradicts this liberty and abolishes the most cogent reasons for revolt. Thrust into a history that has no superior order, the rebel is caught between the political antinomies of violence and nonviolence; between justice and liberty.

Rebels must renounce violence, for violence is foreign to the reasons that initially motivated them. In actuality, however, they cannot turn away from the world and from history without denying the principles of their rebellion. To ignore history amounts to the same thing as denying reality. "Most certainly the rebel does not destroy the history that surrounds him; it is in terms of this that he attempts to affirm himself. But confronted with it, he feels like the artist confronted with reality; he spurns it without escaping from it" (290). An equally insoluble dilemma arises in the antinomy between justice and freedom. Absolute freedom, which allows the right of the strongest to dominate, confirms the reign of injustice. Absolute justice, on the other hand, by tolerating no contradictions suppresses all freedom.

The Philosophy of Limits

According to Camus, the seemingly ineradicable opposition between the moral demands of revolt and the practical attainments of revolution must be relegated to the realm of absolutes. Problems arise primarily because the rebel has forgotten the limitations of authentic revolt. Absolute freedom mocks at justice just as certainly as absolute justice denies freedom; but to be fruitful, the two ideas must find their limits in each other. "No man considers that his condition is free if it is not at the same time just, nor just unless it is free" (291). And the same reasoning can be applied to violence. Absolute nonviolence is the negative basis of slavery and its acts of violence; systematic violence completely destroys the living community and the existence we receive from it. "To be fruitful, these two ideas must establish final limits. In history, considered as an absolute, violence finds itself legitimized; as a relative risk, it is the cause of a rupture in communication." Camus reasons that it must therefore maintain for the rebel "its provisional character of effraction and must always be bound, if it cannot be avoided, to a personal responsibility and to an immediate risk" (292).

The Law of Moderation

Rebellion, then, at the same time that it brings as awareness of a nature that everyone shares, also brings an awareness of the limits it imposes. To the values previously attained from revolt, Camus now adds the law of moderation, a measure by which to judge all people and all events. Moderation is not the opposite of rebellion. On the contrary, rebellion in itself is moderation, and it "demands, defends, and recreates it throughout history and its eternal disturbances" (301). By measure or moderation, Camus refers to that attitude of mind that opposes and is contrary to excess of any kind. To illustrate his meaning, he points to the deification of history by modern political revolutionaries as an example of such extremism. These revolutionaries have failed precisely because they ignored the essential element of measure. Through their preference for an abstract concept of the individual to an individual of flesh and blood, they committed themselves to a rigid dogmatism that could in no way guarantee the achievement of human values. "Moderation, born of rebellion, can only live by rebellion. It is a perpetual conflict, continually created and mastered by the intelligence. It does not triumph either in the impossible or in the abyss. It finds its equilibrium through them. Whatever we may do, excess will always keep its place in the heart of man, in the place where solitude is found. We all carry within us our places of exile, our crimes and our ravages. But our task is not to unleash them on the world; it is to fight them in ourselves and in others" (301).

In this way Camus posits a way of acting and thinking that is not in conflict with the principles of genuine revolt. The model for emulation lies in neither the metaphysical nor the historical revolt of the post-Christian era, but rather in the Mediterranean tradition that triumphs over abstract ideologies by remaining constantly aware of the tension and moderation that are essential features of revolt. The Mediterranean spirit, in conflict with German ideologies, is ever aware of people as they are and rejects the vague promise of some future utopia in order to assert the present grandeur of life. The true rebels choose the present over the future, the fate of humanity for the delusion of power. They give us an example of the only original rule of life today, "to learn to live and to die, and, in order to be a man, to refuse to be a god" (306).

Evaluation and Criticism

Thus Camus concludes his thorough investigation of revolt in the Western world. Regardless of the faults one may find within the work, it is impossible not to be overwhelmed by Camus's sincerity and intellectual integrity. His discussion of the movement of revolt from the pre-Christian era to modern times is profound, provocative, and essential to an understanding of our historical epoch. It is especially relevant to an American who is troubled by the happenings in this country and abroad. And, as always in a discussion of Camus, the weaknesses of his reasoning—which are criticized in the conclusion of this chapter—are also strangely their strengths. Perhaps it all involves his determination to see both sides of the coin, *l'envers et l'endroit*.

In *L'Homme révolté* Camus's position is not fundamentally different from that of the great Western humanists who preceded him. Although to a traditional humanist the world is not absurd and certain values are absolute, he or she, like Camus, also seeks to construct a valid ethical system without any recourse to a priori principles. Camus begins his search for values in a godless world and rather than accepting any given values, he allows the individual to discover these values through his or her own efforts. Unlike some major existentialist thinkers, Camus never denies the existence of values. To do so would completely negate one of the underlying concepts of his thought. In keeping with the development of his philosophic position up to this time, in *L'Homme révolté* he questions many of the phantom ideologies that prevent human beings from attaining their potential value and obscure them not only from themselves but also from others. In many ways *L'Homme révolté* successfully voices a protest against the unnecessary suffering and injustice inflicted upon people by forces that menace their right to freedom and order; and in this respect, it is a compelling contribution to humanistic scholarship. In substance, however, the essay is perhaps too ambitious in its aims and too ambiguous in its positive recommendations to be completely satisfying. The only practical proposal that Camus makes is to suggest a pre-Marxian form of action in keeping with the attitude of the *meurtriers délicats,* whom he extols here and in the drama *Les Justes.* This seems a somewhat meager reward for the average reader who has patiently followed the development of Camus's reasoning through some rather murky passages. It is easy to become lost in the overwhelming list of people Camus finds necessary to mention to clarify his points. It has been pointed out that in a book of 378 pages, there are references to 160 writers, 96 historical characters, and 20 fictional and mythical characters.[1] The fact that the list includes such powerful and diverse personalities as Milton, Napoleon, Christ, and Henry Ford is baffling enough, but when one realizes that Camus devotes almost equal coverage to such major thinkers as Nietzsche, Marx, and Hegel as he does to such esoteric figures as Sergei Netchaiev, Sergei Sasanov, or Maxim Chigalev, one cannot help but be amazed that the essay retains any degree of continuity or clarity of meaning. Camus is somewhat like the victim of the anecdote Hermann Hesse quotes from Novalis in his novel *Steppenwolf.* " 'Most men will not swim before they are able to.' Is not that witty? Naturally, they won't swim! They are born for the solid earth, not for the water. And naturally they won't think. They are made for life, not for thought. Yes, and he who thinks, what's more, he who makes thought his business, he may go far in it, but he has bartered the solid earth for the water all the same, and one day he will drown."[2] Thus the moral intention of *L'Homme révolté* is often confused by or even lost in a mass of ideological and historical detail, and like the victim in Hesse's anecdote, Camus and the reader of his essay can easily drown in an overabundance of exoticism.

There are other weaknesses that are equally bothersome to the reader who searches for a clearly defined argument in *L'Homme révolté.* The essay has frequently been compared to *Le Mythe de Sisyphe;* indeed, Camus himself refers the reader to his earlier writings on the absurd. In many ways *L'Homme révolté* does recapitulate all of his previous work. From the earliest writings to the present essay, he depicts a world that is hazardous, uncertain, and ever changing. Over and over again from the confrontation between a desire for coherence and the irrationality of the world, the absurd is reborn, and in Camus's plays and novels, he is able to fuse human emotion, abstract ideas, and action through his art; but the fusion that is so skillfully and effectively handled in his creative writings becomes a puzzling and unsatisfactory technique in *L'Homme révolté*.

One way to demonstrate the essay's lack of consistency is to contrast its opening sections with the conclusion. The main section of the book is devoted to an analysis of the unlimited revolt that has dominated the past two centuries leading to the totalitarianism of today. This is the traditional concept of revolt as a protest against violence, excess, and nihilism; or to express it another way, it is the rebels' reaction to some superior power's indifference to their needs and desires. In this sense revolt is a philosophic attitude, for it affirms a positive reaction to a life situation: the world is absurd and the individual reacts. In the conclusion of the book, however, revolt takes on a different meaning. It remains a protest against suffering, but is a political rather than an individual reaction. Revolt is specifically directed against certain dogma of political extremism and the Marxist interpretation of history. In this part of the book, Camus limits the concept of revolt to a historical situation and makes no attempt to explain the relationship between the general philosophic meaning of the term and its narrower, political application. It is as if he saw in his own immediate experience a duplication of the initial impetus that led to a reaction to the absurd, but he gives no reason for the shift he makes from one realm of existence to the other, from the philosophic to the political point of view.

It is also obvious to most readers that the lyrical tone of the last section of the book contrasts sharply to the book's otherwise clear and direct prose. There are possible reasons for this shift in style, but none is completely satisfactory. There is no doubt that Camus's search for an ordered and harmonious society is a personal quest that can offer the rebel no set ethical system. Such a construct would inhibit the rebel's freedom. The rebel must remain free to achieve his or her own destiny within the limits of social necessity and not be committed to any preconceived source of action. For this reason, the mystical quality of the language and the eloquent usage of light and dark as symbols of freedom and enslavement alert the reader to Camus's personal insight. The "Pensée de Midi" is his unique poetic vision of what might be possible to attain in this world, and to present it in direct prose would detract from its intended impact. Yet, in spite of the nobility of Camus's plea for a moderate kind of revolt that will ensure individual and collective freedom, the glaring fact remains that the "Pensée de Midi" does little to clarify the essay's intention. For the individual immersed in the complexities and harsh realities of life, an incantation to the virtues of measure, justice, and nature offers little to cling to. One cannot help but wonder whether Camus too did not sense the inadequacy of his conclusion and choose to couch this inadequacy in the symbol of the Mediterranean spirit.

These obviously negative aspects of the book in no way deterred either its sale or critical attention. Camus was proclaimed the defender of individual rights by French, English, and American critics, and the reception of the book clearly established his position as one of France's most important writers. Sir Herbert Read, Waldo Frank, and Philip Toynbee all praised *L'Homme révolté* as an important intellectual contribution to the understanding of the human condition.[3] Yet, as might be anticipated, there was also strong dissenting criticism of Camus's vague ethical position and extremely personal view of history and politics. Of the many controversial discussions that were stimulated by the ideas contained in the book, the most fascinating—certainly the most publicized and significant—involved Camus himself and Jean-Paul Sartre.

The Camus-Sartre Controversy

At the origin of the open clash between Camus and Sartre, which finally broke in the August 1952 issue of *Les Temps Modernes,* is an article that appeared five months earlier in *La Nouvelle Critique.* In April of 1952, over five months after the publication of *L'Homme révolté,* Pierre Hervé, who at that time was a member of the Communist party, wrote an article in which he alleged that Camus had no interest in either colonial affairs or the dangers of nuclear warfare.[4] The entire article contained many equally ridiculous accusations and undoubtedly would have been ignored and forgotten had Jean Lebar not noted in *France-Observateur* that Hervé's criticism was a quite "remarkable" study. For some inexplicable reason, this innocent enough adjective was misread by Camus as "belle" (favorable), an adjective that would have indicated Lebar's admiration for Hervé's opinions. Camus wrote an indignant letter to the *France-Observateur* in which he demanded that Lebar's statement be withdrawn. There was, of course, no withdrawal for an error that Camus himself had made; and the incident, along with Camus's general attitude at this time, gave Sartre an excellent opportunity to attack Camus not only on philosophic and political grounds but also on the personal grounds of aloofness and haughtiness. With a degree of justification, Sartre felt that Camus had become overconscious of his role as spokesman for the French intellectuals and in a scathing remark questioned, "Tell me, Camus, by what strange miracle can one not criticise your books without depriving humanity of its reasons for living?"[5]

Unfortunately, this taunting tone runs through a great deal of the discussion of Camus's ideas by both Sartre and his disciple Francis Jeanson. In May of 1952, Jeanson published a long and highly critical review of *L'Homme révolté* in *Les Temps Modernes* in which he accused Camus of failing to face real issues. Jeanson maintained that Camus sought to remain outside history, that he ignored human struggles in favor of metaphysical concepts, and that through his emphasis upon the crimes committed by revolutionaries and his attack upon Marxism and Stalinism, he allied himself with the smug bourgeoisie and reenforced the ideas it wished to hear.

Three months after the Jeanson article appeared, *Les Temps Modernes* published a sixteen-page letter of self-defense written by Camus at Sartre's invitation. In the same issue were letters of replies from both Sartre and Jeanson. The actual debate centered on the men's disagreement about the political position of a left-wing intellectual. Sartre maintained that only through support of the Communist party, and an active attempt to orient it from within, could an honest course of political action be followed. Although he in no way found the party the perfect answer to the problems of the working class, he insisted that "in order to deserve the right to influence men who struggle, one must start by participating in their battle. One must start by accepting a lot of things, if one wants to attempt to change a few."[6] Camus challenged the efficacy of Sartre's position and called for a new orientation of leftist intellectual thought through his analysis of the degradation of the ideologies of the French Revolution and the Communist party. He further asserted that no honest movement could have anything to do with Stalinism.

Regardless of the political issues involved, the argument ultimately concerned the philosophic differences between Camus and Sartre. Sartre refuses any prior human nature and sees men and women as the sum of all of their acts. We are in history and through our actions in time we create values that can come into being only through an active engagement in political activity. Although Camus agrees with Sartre that we exist physically in history, at the same time he also believes that we can transcend history by participating in what he calls the human spirit. In his letter to Sartre, he draws attention to a basic contradiction in Sartre's position. "Only prophetic Marxism (or a philosophy of eternity)," he says, "could justify the pure and simple rejection of my thesis." He then asks directly, "but how can such views be upheld in your magazine without contradiction? Because, after all, if there is no human end that can be made into a norm of value, how can history have a definable meaning? On the other hand, if history has meaning why shouldn't man make of it his end?"[7]

These questions remained unanswered. Sartre replied to Camus that "man participates in history in order to pursue the eternal. He uncovers universal values in the concrete action which he performs with a specific purpose in view." But his statement does little to clarify the issue at hand. In fact, as John Cruickshank points out, Sartre's use of such concepts as "the eternal" and "universal values" seems to approach a position amazingly close to Camus's.[8] Without delving into the complexities of the discussion between the two men,[9] the most disappointing aspect of the quarrel is that neither Camus nor Sartre, who were both sincerely involved in a search for human betterment, could establish a common ground. Certainly neither won the argument. There is something humanly compelling in Sartre's restless desire to improve our lives through immediate and direct action. On the other hand, one must admire Camus's attempt to do something that Sartre does not. In *L'Homme révolté,* because he felt intellectually responsible for his commitments, he endeavors to account for his position on current political ideologies. There is little doubt that Camus's position is the more idealistic of the two—a patient search for values is always a logically superior basis for action than is a fatal commitment to a militant ideology—however, the question remains unanswered whether or not an individual can take time daily to reexamine and to redefine his or her political position.

Conclusion

The intellectual controversy that arose following the publication of *L'Homme révolté* monopolized Camus's time well into 1952 and usurped the energy that could have been devoted to his creative writing. For Camus, however, there was no escape from his involvement. Throughout his career, he was constantly and passionately involved not only with what he thought and wrote but also with the way people received and reacted to his ideas. Unlike some writers and philosophers, Camus could never divorce himself from his writings. Whether he wrote of death, of longing, or of revolt, it was always his death, his longing, or his revolt about which he spoke. This intense and often painful relationship between the man and his work is both a weakness and a strength. It is a weakness because the personal and poetic qualities of his writings are frequently difficult to pinpoint and often, as in the "Pensée de midi," they are so personal that they defy criticism. Conversely, the personal diligence with which he develops his experiences into a philosophy is so honest that the reader cannot resist working with Camus until they both attain a conclusion—now far removed from the initial personal experience—that is logically and humanly tenable. Sartre, too, in spite of their quarrel, must have felt some of this same fascination for Camus when he wrote in his tribute to him: "That man on the move questioned us, was himself a question seeking its reply; he lived *in the middle of a long life;* for us, for him, for the men who maintain order and for those who reject it, it was important for him to break his silence, for him to decide, for him to conclude."[10]

Chapter Eight
The Other Side of the Coin
1951–1956

Nineteen hundred and fifty-six, the year of the publication of *La Chute* (*The Fall*), marks Camus's return to imaginative writing. But the years between 1951 and 1956 were not silent ones. There are the essays that make up the collections of *Actuelles II* (Chronicles) and *L'Eté;* there are the translations, adaptations, and productions of plays by Calderón de la Barca, Pierre Larivey, Dino Buzzati, Faulkner, and Dostoevski; and there are the prefaces to the works of Oscar Wilde and Martin du Gard. Although many may have wondered if Camus had not lost himself in the mass of ideological and historical detail incorporated in *L'Homme révolté,* the works that were published during this time indicate that he was consciously limiting his literary activities to a personal and public clarification of what he had already written. The secret, inner conflict that he had to resolve before he could again assert his powers as a creative writer involved his own understanding of his role as an artist in the twentieth century. He had to free himself from doctrinaire imperatives and political commitment to be able to return to his initial conviction that "the supreme aim of art is to confound all judges, to abolish all accusations, and to justify everything, life and mankind, in a light which is the light of beauty only because it is the light of truth."[1]

L'Eté

To rediscover his own "light of beauty," Camus first had to rediscover himself. *L'Homme révolté* marked a stage in his thought beyond which it was difficult for him to progress. He needed to know if he could again find the source of joy, love, and light that originally had protected him from despair. The truth of his pilgrimage to self-understanding is expressed in the eight lyrical essays published under the title of *L'Eté* (*Summer*). These essays, written between 1939 and 1951, are dominated by the emphasis on beauty, happiness, and art that characterized his earlier writings, and they represent Camus's return to a lyrical meditation on the richness of the universe and the happiness of life that is reminiscent of *L'Envers et l'endroit* and *Noces*. The crisis of the war had passed and Camus felt that he could temporarily put aside the arid arguments of political controversy and resume his search for a personally fulfilling life. In the preface to the 1957 edition of *L'Envers et l'endroit* he declared his intention to begin all over again, to go all the way back to this first work, which contained all the contradictions, the ambiguities, the two facets of light and shadow, innocence and guilt that characterized his world of life and creativity. Given Camus's manner of gradually developing his own philosophic position, it is not at all surprising that after the intense questioning that underlies the thought of *L'Homme révolté* he returned to his initial artistic impulse. The investigations of the political evils of his epoch left little room for the impassioned appreciation of life that runs through his less didactic writings.

La Chute

We have seen that each stage in his thought is a movement toward a certain intellectual grasp of life. Unlike a systematic philosopher such as Sartre, Camus felt his way into his philosophy by first examining an aspect of experience on the personal level and then expanding this personal experience into a universal truth that would better illuminate the human condition. Thus just as *L'Etranger* foreshadowed a philosophic position that was further clarified in *Le Mythe de Sisyphe,* the idea of limits inherent in *La Peste,* but not fully developed until *L'Homme révolté,* corrected and defined the initial position. It is from this deliberate self-limitation to a unified idea that Camus draws his power as an artist and a thinker. His complex thought process allows him to experiment, to limit, and eventually to evolve a philosophic position that without ever negating the initial impulse constantly corrects and refines it. In his essay "L'Artiste et son temps," Camus said that "the aim of art is . . . first to understand."[2] It was his desire to understand the complexities of life that led him through the manifold stages of his developing thought, and it is exactly this same characteristic that compelled him to write the most controversial of all his books, *La Chute.*

In a fashion reminiscent of Samuel Coleridge's Ancient Mariner, Jean-Baptiste Clamence, the monologist of *La Chute,* awaits his oppor-

tunity to involve a stranger in conversation and to confess his past
crimes and weaknesses. His engaging tale is told with cynical wit and
scheming complicity. As the narration progresses through six short
sections, the reader soon realizes that it is he or she whom Clamence has
chosen as his audience. Clamence begins telling his story in a cheap
waterfront bar called Mexico City and located in the slum section of
Amsterdam. He had been an envied and highly esteemed Parisian
lawyer. He had defended the poor and the victimized and had enjoyed
the pleasure of knowing that he was on the right side. He was handsome, an excellent dancer, a marvelous conversationalist, and a gener-
ous and courteous man. He was, in other words, a pillar of bourgeois
society. Everything seemed to tell him that the happiness he so completely enjoyed was authorized "by some higher decree."[3] Then one
night as he was returning quite late from a visit to one of his mistresses,
something happened that shattered his moral complacency and self-
esteem. As he crossed the Seine on the Pont Royal, he passed a slim
young woman dressed in black. She was leaning over the bridge railing
and staring into the river. After he had gone on some fifty yards he
heard the sound "of a body striking the water" (70). He stopped,
listened, and heard a cry repeated several times. He stood motionless
and then went away, but he could never forget the suicide he might
have prevented. The memory of this moment of cowardice was kept
alive by a mysterious sound of laughter that had "come from nowhere,
unless from the water" (39). From this time on Clamence began to see
within himself the vanity, "the handsome wax figure," the emptiness
that he was. As he progressed from memory to memory he gradually
discovered that his former good deeds had been done only for the sake
of popular approval. He could remember no moral or courteous act that
he had performed when there were no witnesses to applaud his actions.
Overcome by the hollowness of his existence, he decided to immunize
himself against the laughter that haunted him by immersing himself in
various forms of debauchery. One day aboard a ship, however, he
perceived a black speck on the steel-gray ocean and was reminded of a
drowning person. He then realized that he could not escape the cry that
had sounded over the Seine many years before, and that he had to
submit to and admit a guilt that would await him "on seas and rivers,
everywhere" (108). Consciously aware of the "fundamental duplicity of
the human being" (84) and the fact that "the keenest of human torments is to be judged without a law" (117), Clamence dedicated himself to the profession of a judge-penitent. From that decisive moment

onward, he made endurable the duplicity he had discovered by persuading his listeners that they too were guilty of the same amazing and horrifying acts. Only by judging himself could he escape the judgment of others, and only through his own confession could the image he creates of himself "become a mirror" to his contemporaries and proclaim the inescapable guilt of all people:

Covered with ashes, tearing my hair, my face scored by clawing, but with piercing eyes, I stand before all humanity recapitulating my shames without losing sight of the effect I am producing, and saying: "I was the lowest of the low." Then imperceptibly I pass from the "I" to the "we." When I get to "This is what we are," the trick has been played and I can tell them off. I am like them, to be sure; we are in the soup together. However, I have a superiority in that I know it and this gives me the right to speak. You see the advantage, I am sure. The more I accuse myself, the more I have a right to judge you. Even better, I provoke you into judging yourself, and this relieves me of that much of the burden. (140)

Relationship of *La Chute* to Camus's Other Writings

The action of *La Chute* emphasizes certain aspects of human behavior that have not heretofore been investigated by Camus. In all of his writings from *L'Envers et l'endroit* to *L'Homme révolté*, there has been an underlying assumption of human innocence. Camus has consistently defended the innocence of men and women against those ideologies and theologies that attempt to corrupt this innocence and treat them as if guilty. In *Le Mythe de Sisyphe*, in *L'Homme révolté*, as well as in the more imaginative writings, evil was always considered an outside force. In *L'Etranger*, the structure of society was seen to be more at fault than Meursault; in *La Peste*, humanity in general was presented as the innocent victim of events; and much of the critical commentary surrounding *L'Homme révolté* resulted from Camus's oversimplification of the problem of evil. There he blamed the crimes committed in the name of communism upon the philosopher Hegel. Realizing the one-sided aspect of his argument up to this time, Camus sought to correct his reasoning in *La Chute*. If, as he previously argued, the individual is innocent, then the natural assumption is that all men and women are innocent. The laws of logic dictate that if all are innocent, there can be no human-created evil to resist. Obviously evil does exist, and people exist who create the conditions against which the rebel revolts. Camus reasons in a way similar to Sartre that although the subjective "I" views the self as innocent, the day must arrive when this subjective "I" perceives another "I" who also considers him or herself as innocent. Up to the moment of confrontation between the "I" and an "other," it is possible to speak of evil as outside the self or in "others," but after the confrontation the "I" becomes aware that to the "others" he or she is an "other." The "I" then recognizes both subjective innocence and objective guilt. It is this double nature—certainly not an original concept— that Camus now turns to and investigates in *La Chute*. His concern with the guilty evildoer, Jean-Baptiste Clamence, as opposed to the innocent rebels, who up to this time have been his central concern, represents a turning point in his thought and a progression to a more complete, if less optimistic, understanding of human nature.

Interpretation

There are innumerable references to duality throughout the book. The title itself suggests that there was a state of innocence before the fall into the hell of present-day Amsterdam. The city is used as an artistic device in much the same way that Oran was employed in *La Peste*. Here, in contrast to the blazing sunlight of Oran, but nonetheless reflecting the same artistic intent, the rain and mist of Amsterdam create a psychological atmosphere that emphasizes the uncertainty of the ideas expressed in the book. At Amsterdam, the Zuydersee of which no one knows "where it begins or ends" (97), the canals with their "stagnant waters" and "smell of dead leaves", and even the people who "are here and elsewhere" all reflect the modern hell of ambiguity in which it is impossible to distinguish between guilt and innocence. Unlike the innocent rebels of *L'Etranger* and *La Peste,* there is no clarity for the people of this northern world, no blending into a perfect harmony with life. They can distinguish neither on the physical nor on the moral level. Their lives are not ones of blindness, but of unclarity. In much the same way that we might awkwardly stumble and fall in foggy half-light, the people of this modern world cannot intellectually perceive their ideals. Theirs is an existence of eternal doubt, distrust, and fall. There is no doctrine of redemption and no law to guide them. Their fall is not the Christian fall from innocence, but rather a fall from innocence that is self-inflicted without any reference to law. Clamence says that "he who clings to a law does not fear the judgment that reinstates him in an order he believes in. But the keenest of human torments is to be judged without a law" (117).

Two closely related episodes in the novel serve a double purpose. They both clarify the keen suffering that Clamence inflicts upon himself and they also help to define Camus's special use of the word *fall*. We are already familiar with the first crucial event that shattered Clamence's Parisian paradise. Although unaware of it at the time, the evening that he ignored the cry of the slim young woman on the Pont Royal ushered in his state of guilt. The second central moment, derived from the first, took place two or three years later, and again occurred on a bridge over the river Seine. Clamence was happy within himself. He had had a good day and was enjoying a vast feeling of power and completion. At the moment he was about to light "a cigarette of satisfaction" (39), a laugh burst out behind him. He wheeled around suddenly but no one was there. He turned back and again heard the laughter a little farther off "as if it were going downstream" (39). This laugh, which Clamence "believed" he heard, is the event that shatters his complacency. Even the most casual reader notices similarities between this event and the earlier one. There are the similarities of setting, scene, and time: a bridge, deserted or becoming so, darkness, and autumn. In both instances Clamence is alone, satisfied, and happy. During the events a noise is heard—a laugh, a cry—behind Clamence, from an unknown source—an invisible person, an unidentified woman—a noise repeated, still from behind him, which floats down the river. After the events, Clamence's immediate reaction is a kind of immobilization or paralysis, followed by parallel nervous reactions of skin and heart. As if in a dream, the second experience is a distortion at the subconscious level of the former one. The suicide that Clamence thought he had forgotten was essentially reproduced for him when he stumbled upon the set of circumstances with which he subconsciously associated it.

At this moment Clamence must consciously face his previous action. He can no longer ignore his responsibility as a human being. Although he endeavors to lose himself in debauchery and to escape his guilt, he cannot. He goes through a long period of revolt against the implications of the laugh, but when he thinks that his efforts to avoid responsibility have finally succeeded, when, through debauchery, the last phase of his revolt, he reaches a state of existence so foggy that "the laughter became so muffled that eventually [he] ceased to notice it" (106), he is caught off guard by a speck on the ocean and is forced to acknowledge the event of the suicide and resign himself to his guilt. He must finally admit that he was responsible for his actions the evening he chose to ignore the woman on the bridge. Up to that time he had acted in accord with a set of values established by the society he lived in. But on that particular evening he was alone, there was no witness to applaud his acts, and on that evening when he ignored the plaint of the drowning woman, he chose himself above the virtuous code he had been following. It was at that time that he placed complete responsibility upon himself and rejected his Parisian paradise. The total implication of the decision is not realized until the second bridge episode. From that point onward, Clamence moved toward full consciousness. Camus entangles him in an intriguing psychological mesh. Once the initial act has been committed, Clamence cannot ever again regain his former state of innocence. It might be argued that his fall into the awareness of his freedom and responsibility is a fall into a better state than his earlier unconscious innocence, but the fact remains that the condition has changed and that Clamence finds it almost impossible to face himself and to bring his personal life into some sort of accord with his understanding of himself and the world.

Comparison of Clamence to Meursault and Rieux

The fall for Camus is a fall into an awareness of the truth of our position in the twentieth century. This book, like the others, entails a biting criticism of the laws that govern and judge human behavior. Because of this factor, the early Clamence has much in common with Camus's other heroes. He personifies that aspect of society that sat in judgment upon Meursault. Clamence, before his fall, was the most eloquent pleader for the accused and oppressed. He was the example par excellence of the formidable bourgeoisie, which defends the letter of the law without ever questioning its morality. But it is Clamence after his fall who is most interesting to us, and it is in his state of guilt that his comparison to Meursault becomes most meaningful.

The difference between Clamence and Meursault here is that Clamence is guilty of an act, unjudged and untried by society, whereas Meursault was tried and judged for an act that in reality he did not commit. In the case of Meursault, society is willing to overlook the fact that he murdered an Arab, but unwilling to ignore his seeming indifference at his mother's wake. It is for his crime of being an outsider to his social milieu that Meursault is finally sentenced to death, but in his last moments of life Meursault is granted the luxury of personal happiness. He is able to discover and enjoy an inner satisfaction that Clamence never achieves. Clamence's crime, legally, is no crime at all; but his awareness of his guilt, his failure to measure up to human expectations, is acute enough to plague his conscience and to force him into a state of self-inflicted punishment. The contrast might be expressed in still another way. Through his trial Meursault is awakened to life and the splendors of the universe, whereas Clamence, through his self-imposed judgment, is awakened to an awareness of his other self and the hell of modern men and women.

In many ways Clamence rounds out the flatness of Meursault's character. He learns that he himself partakes of and contributes to the world's evil. Evil is not something outside himself, and he assumes the burden of his responsibility. Meursault never faced the fact that regardless of the circumstances, he did pull the trigger and fire the shot that took another's life. He never faced the fact that he transgressed the limits of acceptable human behavior.

In a less dramatic sense, the early Clamence also resembles Dr. Rieux. He, like Rieux, acts in accordance with the laws of his society and from one point of view, Clamence can be seen as a benefactor and healer. He helps the poor, aids the crippled, and defends the unfortunate. He, again like Rieux, subscribes to no orthodox religion, and his own estimation of himself as "fully and simply a man" echoes Rieux's interest in "being a man." Although Rieux has none of the haughtiness of Clamence, and little of his conceit, they do share a certain desire to do a job well within the framework of an absurd universe. As many critics have suggested, *La Chute* may be read as Camus's own criticism of the human innocence implicit in *La Peste,* for until Clamence became fully conscious of his impure motives, he had been living as a legal equivalent of Dr. Rieux.

Regardless of the similarities between Clamence and the earlier heroes, there is one element that clearly distinguishes him from his literary ancestors. Clamence is overwhelmingly dissatisfied with his role in the universe. He discovers neither the splendors of Meursault's world nor the magnificence of Rieux's men. He only discovers his own middle-class hell with its "streets filled with shop signs and no way of explaining oneself" (47). He is acutely aware of his own and of humanity's shortcomings, but he is able to do nothing about them. In a striking way Clamence is not evil incarnate but is rather the incarnation of twentieth-century hopes and joys gone astray. Here again Camus has taken an individual experience and expanded it to reflect a universal truth. Clamence as "the image of all and of no one" is the concrete example of the suffering of men and women within the twentieth-century bourgeois society. There are no values for them to catch hold of. The wars and the events following the wars have left little of enduring worth. Clamence cannot find the quiet joys of Meursault and Rieux. He knows nothing of the friendship that Rieux experienced with Tarrou. He only knows that the "earth is dark, . . . the coffin thick, and the shroud opaque" (74). He can find no certainty in anything. Yet, he admits that he loves life, and that fact is not only, as he says, his "real weakness," but it is also his real tragedy. Clamence is truly the man adrift. He is conscious of his own weaknesses and in turn he bears the weight of the painful consciousness of the weakness of the entire world. That night on the bridge he foresook his innocence and his virtue, and became free. By his own admission, however, his freedom is unbearable. By implication Camus places all twentieth-century men and women in much the same position as Clamence. None can find a law to cling to that will regain the lost paradise. All suffer the consequences of their moment in history, and in order to make life have some meaning they surmount the agony of moral uncertainty and horror of freedom by finding others who share their guilt. Clamence is modern man, searching for lost values and setting himself up as a god. Only by judging others and making them aware of their guilt can he in some small way endure his freedom. Clamence tells us that "on the bridges of Paris I . . . learned that I was afraid of freedom" (136). The fact that he chose his freedom the night he ignored the woman on the bridge in no way makes the burden of this freedom any easier to bear. In order to bear life at all, he must find others to share his guilt, for only by judging others can he lighten the weight of the judgment he has placed upon himself.

Seen in this manner, Clamence takes his place alongside Meursault, Rieux, and Camus's other characters to present a composite picture of modern men and women. Clamence, the lawyer, could as easily be Clamence the doctor, the teacher, the philosopher. His function, like that of many learned and intellectual people, is to perceive the dangers of present society, to point out these dangers, and to offer a few positive suggestions to better the situation. Clamence proceeds a step further than most twentieth-century intellectuals in that he does insert the idea of some distant hope. The faint hope that Clamence offers stems from his belief that through self-judgment, he can attain an understanding of and prepare the way to the rediscovery of an old innocence and a new law that will protect this innocence. By living through the hell that is his, he never loses sight of the islands that hold out the promise of a brighter future, the islands of innocence and redemption. Amsterdam is, after all, the "last circle," the densest and darkest of Hell, and although Clamence has "learned to be satisfied with understanding," the implied hope exists that the rest of humanity may someday progress beyond satisfaction to an attainment of "the light, the mornings, the holy innocence of those who forgive themselves" (145).

Autobiographical Aspects of *La Chute*

The duality of Clamence's character is underlined by almost every sentence of *La Chute,* and it affects the reader's reaction to this strange but familiar confession. Many critics have seen Camus directly reflected in his fictional character, and there is no doubt that Camus used much of his own experience in creating his modern-day John the Baptist. Camus's personal charm, his consciousness of the elegance of language, his opposition to judges and unfeeling legalism, his concern with religion and politics are all reflected in his portrayal of Clamence. But in spite of these obvious connections between the author and his creation, the book remains one of the least revealing confessions ever written. According to Clamence, "authors of confessions write especially to avoid confessing, to tell nothing of what they know" (120), and his statement in many ways serves as an astute judgment on the critics who strain to find a too exacting parallel between Camus and Clamence. In his portrait of Clamence, Camus is not so much interested in creating an individual as he is in using a particular individual as the embodiment of an idea. Clamence shares a moral self-consciousness with Camus that everyone expresses at one time or another. Ours is after all the century of the "I," the epoch that finds it difficult to love, the age in which communication is a one-sided authoritarian affair. *La Chute* further suggests that it is a time of inaction, in which "words, words, words" resound against a cold, empty backdrop of gray. Ours is also an era that in its emphasis on the "I, I, I" leads the individual in his or her most despondent moments to be seduced into agreement with Clamence's desire "to block the door of the closed little universe of which I am the king, the pope, and the judge" (128). All of these ideas, generally stated here, but more precisely dis-

cussed in the text of *La Chute*, must be common property to the majority
of thinking men and women. If not, the effectiveness of the book would
be lost to all but those few who have an intimate knowledge of Camus's
biography. Camus, himself aware of the limiting aspect that a strictly
biographical interpretation would impose upon *La Chute*, prefaced the
English edition with a quotation from Mikhail Lermontov: "Some were
dreadfully insulted, and quite seriously, to have held up as a model such
an immoral character as *A Hero of Our Time;* others shrewdly noticed that
the author had portrayed himself and his acquaintances. . . . *A Hero of
Our Time,* gentlemen, is in fact a portrait, but not of an individual; it is
the aggregate of the vices of our whole generation in their fullest
expression."

Jean-Baptiste Clamence

It is true that beyond these obvious biographical and fictional parallels between Clamence and Camus, the reader totally ignorant of Camus's personal life and thought is drawn into a much broader and more
significant portrayal than that of an individual man in the 1950s.
Clamence is the mirror of "all and of no one," for his tragedy, the
tragedy of a man without values, in desperate search for something—
almost anything—that will give meaning to his life, is the tragedy of
many of us. The pat answers, indifferently meted out by the church and
the state, really offer no solace once they are challenged. Within a
world that lives in constant fear of total destruction, we need an answer
that can be tangibly illustrated. Meursault found this answer in the
warmth and beauties of the Mediterranean sun. He needed nothing
beyond the present moment and the promise of a never-ending succession of moments. Rieux found his answer in human dignity. But for
Clamence, placed in the same bourgeois, bureaucratic world, there is
no universal splendor and no human warmth. He is one of the less
fortunate who cannot find satisfaction. He longs for his lost innocence
but is aware of his guilt and cannot find any noble solution to his
dilemma. This almost totally pessimistic portrayal of us as creatures of
duplicity whose bad faith can destroy even our best intentions does not
negate the truths of Camus's earlier writings any more than *La Peste*
negated the absurd universe of *L'Etranger*. What a person can accomplish against collective evil is one issue; what one can do to control the
evil of an individual human conscience is quite another.

In *La Chute* Camus leads his reader into a world that in many ways ⌐ more easily recognized than the worlds of either *L'Etranger* or *La Peste*. It is our world without illusions. He evokes an intellectual desert, peopled by men and women conscious of their estrangement from an incomprehensible world, and he takes us to this desert, enclosed by a fog "compounded of neon, gin, and mint" (13). There in the seeming refuge of the Mexico City bar, he introduces us to the monologist, Jean-Baptiste Clamence, the "empty prophet for shabby times" (117).

For five days we listen to this man who proclaims himself to be "the image of all and of no one" (139). We are shocked by his single sentence characterization of us as fornicators and readers of newspapers (6–7); we are amused by his snobbish use of language and literary allusions (5, 14); we are enticed by his confession of being "the lowest of the low" (140); and we are seduced by his words, words, words until finally we realize that we have become entrapped by his rambling confession into recognizing ourselves behind his "both lifelike and stylized mask" (139). This self-appointed prophet, who inhabits the limbo of those who have betrayed others and themselves, shouts that we are the same as he, if only we will listen to his voice crying out in the modern desert. He lives in a world without a Christ, without an eternal Father, and without justice. He is a Sadducee who proclaims the basic law of repentance in bitter and mocking language. He is truly the mirror of modern men and women who without God search in torment to fill the void created by His absence. In his attempt to give form to chaos, Clamence explores the contradictions of the human dilemma and attempts to mold these contradictions into something that will give meaning and purpose to existence.

In Amsterdam where the sea steams like laundry, Camus creates a psychological atmosphere in which guilt and innocence, pride and humility, and comedy and deadly seriousness are difficult to distinguish one from the other. This ambiguity of atmosphere underscores the duplicity of Clamence as a judge-penitent, as a man whose sense of superiority over others is constantly poisoned by his awareness of his own guilt; but more than that, it creates an atmosphere in which Camus can rebel against the natural formlessness of life and give both life and history a unity and a coherence that it lacks in our experience of it. In *L'Homme révolté* Camus argues that art corrects natural disorder and provides us with a refuge from the all-consuming movement of time. The writing of novels is one way to give life the fixed and irredeemable quality we long for but find unattainable. In *La Chute*

Camus artistically stops the humanly absurd and irrational onslaught of time. He tempts us with complex allusions to recapture and to reevaluate history in such a way that we can comprehend, if not change, the disorder, contradiction, and intellectual mystification that characterize our time.

Allusions to Other Times and Places in *La Chute*

Anyone familiar with Camus's writings is aware of his fondness for allusions. Often, as Meursault's reading of the newspaper account of *Le Malentendu* in *L'Etranger* or the reference to Meursault's guilt of indifference in *La Peste,* the allusions merely interconnect these works with the entire body of Camus's literary production and place the actions of the particular novel or drama into a broader context. The allusions in *La Chute* are, however, more complex and frequent. Perhaps the most obvious allusions are those to contemporary Western life, but equally constant are those to the biblical age of John the Baptist and to the enigmatic early Renaissance of the Flemish painters, the Van Eyck brothers, and their Ghent Altarpiece. The allusions are unified by the voice of Jean-Baptiste Clamence and illustrate Camus's belief that art is the total and indistinguishable union of form and content.

The equation of these diverse historical epochs is intentionally done by Camus. In his essay "On the Future of Tragedy," he remarks that "great periods of tragic art occur, in history, during centuries of crucial change, at moments when the lives of whole peoples are heavy both with glory and with menace, when the future is uncertain and the present dramatic. . . . [T]he tragic age always seems to coincide with an evolution in which man, consciously or not, frees himself from an older form of civilization and finds that he has broken away from it without yet having found a new form that satisfies him" (296–98). That Camus believed the mid-twentieth century was such an epoch is established by his comments within the same essay.[4] In a post-Darwinian, post-Marxian, post-Nietzschean, post-Freudian era no one could any longer doubt that Western men and women had broken from older forms and had not as yet found a new form to satisfy them. The point that Camus wished to convey to the reader of *La Chute* was that such an age need not be empty. Quite the contrary, it could be full of hope as well as challenge. To convey his convictions, Camus had to devise a narrative form that would gently lead his reader to draw analogies between the present moment and history. Mid-twentieth-century men and women needed to be conscious of their unique advantage. Seldom in Western history had the combination of events invited us to begin anew and search for a "new form" to give life meaning.

That Camus succeeded in *La Chute* in giving artistic form to his exploration into the contradictory and unreconciled facts of the human dilemma becomes apparent through an analysis of his skillful manipulation of a triple time level. Through the central character of Jean-Baptiste Clamence, the present time of modern-day Amsterdam is seen in relation to the historical time of John the Baptist and to the Renaissance period of the Ghent Altarpiece. As in a symphony, the theme of the twentieth-century bourgeois world of Clamence blends into the theme of the biblical world of John the Baptist, and both are highlighted by the theme of the Ghent Altarpiece that runs throughout the novel. As an image of the Renaissance, the altarpiece is used by Camus to unite the central image of John the Baptist with the potentially new Renaissance of the twentieth century.

The game of allusion that Camus plays with his reader recalls Mark Twain's comment that "you can find in a text whatever you bring, if you will stand between it and the mirror of your imagination."[5] The statement makes equally frightening demands upon the artist who creates as it does upon the reader who responds to that creation. The artist must stimulate the reader's imagination by extracting from the natural disorder of the world a unity that is satisfying to the mind and the heart of the reader. The reader, in turn, must not only open his or her mind to those stimuli, but must bring to the text sufficient knowledge and experience so that what is discovered in his or her "mirror of imagination" may be translated into clear, precise thought. That Camus was well aware of the necessity of exercising selectivity and control over reality in order to create an imaginary world that his reader could identify with is apparent in his simultaneous evocation of the three separate time periods under discussion.

John the Baptist

The average reader of *La Chute* can be expected to be familiar with both the bourgeois world of the 1950s and the biblical figure of John the Baptist, and will have little difficulty relating to the direct and indirect allusions to each throughout *La Chute*. Clamence makes numerous references to practically every facet of contemporary Western life. Not only are the momentous events of the past fifty years recalled, but even the mundane activities of the men and women who people this self-made hell of a modern world are at least fleetingly alluded to.[6] Whether the reader's point of reference is social, political, historical, or philosophic, he or she recognizes the world of *La Chute* as his or her own world of discomfort and discontent.

The same sort of general statement may be made in respect to John the Baptist. Although most readers may not be aware that during the century in which John was born great forces clashed in Palestine and circumstances made adjustment to pressures extremely difficult, they are aware that John is the last of the Old Testament prophets and the annunciator of the New. Historically the basic conflict of the first century was between the principles and practices of Roman rule and the institutions and ideals of the Jewish nation as a sovereign people under God. Equally important, however, were the tensions created in the social and economic spheres. Here the conflict centered about the ambitious program of urbanization and of capitalistic enterprise by which the Herodians sought to bring a relatively simple and self-sufficient agrarian Palestine into line with the highly industrial and urban civilization of the Augustan era. In the field of religious life and thought, too, there was turmoil caused by opportunism on the one side and escape from reality on the other.

For John to live as he did in the trough of the Jordan valley, enclosed by precipitous mountains that radiate the sun's heat, meant to separate himself from the normal and planned life of others. Such separation implies a profound disregard of and simultaneously a deep revulsion against the established cultural order. For these reasons, it cannot be casual in origin, but must have its roots in some bitter experience that turned him permanently aside from the normal course of human life. If judged by the violence of John's reaction, the roots of his alienation from the life of his day had to lie very deep.

Although the facts of John's life may not be so well known as are the events of the immediate historical past, the allusion to John the Baptist in *La Chute* is sufficiently clear that the reader recognizes the historical John the Baptist in "the empty prophet for shabby times." Both the prophet John and the Sadducee Jean-Baptiste Clamence wander alone on a desert, tortured by their peoples' offenses; and while they prophesy the coming day "that burneth like a furnace," they demand repentance and baptism from their hearers. Again, here in reference to John, as in the earlier reference to the modern world, there are sufficient allusions throughout the narrative that the reader cannot fail to make the association among Jean-Baptiste Clamence, John the Baptist, and him or herself.

The Ghent Altarpiece

The allusions to the Ghent Altarpiece are somewhat more complex and indirect than those to either the contemporary world or to John the Baptist. The altarpiece is mentioned in four of the six divisions of the book for a total of five times.[7] Camus employs the altarpiece not only to recall the general ambience of a particular period or a specific person, but perhaps more significantly, the altarpiece becomes a symbolic and aesthetic focus underlying the many layers of meaning in *La Chute*.

Camus was fascinated by Renaissance painting.[8] The northern Renaissance is particularly interesting to anyone concerned with those moments in history "when the future is uncertain and the present dramatic." The Ghent Altarpiece was completed in 1432, a time that is not only transitional in the Western world at large but is specifically important in the realm of the fine arts. The intuitive and instinctive in art that had produced the naive but nonetheless real expression of Christianity's grand theme in the Middle Ages was being challenged by the academic point of view. Art was being subjected to theory and rules, and reduced in scale to the intellectual possibilities, divorced from the individual religious experience, of its creator.

The shift in emphasis from an acknowledged universal Christian truth to a particular individual's perception of that same truth brought art down from the cosmic unity of the art of the cathedral into the vagaries of the art of the marketplace. Although most art continued to be concerned with religious subject matter, the clear symbolism of the earlier art of the cathedral became obscured behind a preoccupation with concrete facts. As interest developed in individuals and the material environment that defined them, religious significance became blurred. Fifteenth-century art, in the north in particular, was given over to naturalistic recording of detail. Saints and Divine Persons were certainly not relegated to a secondary position, but their domination of the scene was often thrown out of focus because of the artist's exaggerated attention to minute detail.

In the midst of this obscuring of the imaginative side of realism by an apparent surrender to the merely natural, the unmistakable quest for the infinite emerges as well. The paradox that resulted from the tension created by these two forces at play is what makes the art of the period

Jan van Eyck: exterior of the Ghent Altarpiece, St. Bavo's Cathedral, Ghent, Belgium.
Courtesy of the Belgium Tourist Office, New York.

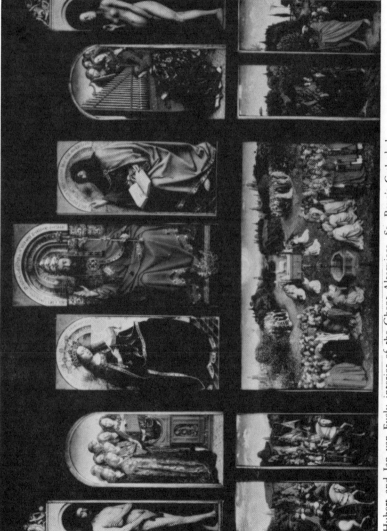

Hubert and Jan van Eyck: interior of the Ghent Altarpiece, St. Bavo's Cathedral, Ghent, Belgium. *Courtesy of the Belgium Tourist Office, New York.*

fascinating from an aesthetic as well as philosophic point of view. In many of the paintings and altarpieces, the neutral backgrounds that sufficed for the symbolic composition of the earlier medieval style are pierced to give a vista into the unknown. To the realistic viewpoint, these vistas are indispensable. To the spiritual viewpoint, these same vistas replace the unlimited effect of space that once was conveyed by the cathedrals' soaring interiors and vast windows.[9]

The Ghent Altarpiece belongs to this art world. In the altarpiece, by juxtaposing the minutiae of an interior with a vast almost cosmic panorama, the Van Eycks simultaneously realized, and in a sense reconciled, the infinitely small and infinitely large, the world of the microcosm and the world of the macrocosm. It is the successful blending of these two worlds into an organic whole that accounts for much of the altarpiece's reputation.

The altarpiece is a polyptych that measures approximately seventeen by eighteen feet and has twenty irregularly sized panels.[10] Nineteen of the original paintings have survived. In April of 1934 the panels of the "Just Judges" and "St. John the Baptist" were stolen. The "St. John the Baptist" was recovered, but the panel with the "Just Judges" has never been found, and it has been replaced with a replica by J. van der Veken. When the altarpiece is closed, the upper tier of the outer panels includes "The Annunciation" and, in the lunettes above it, elaborate little vaulted chambers contain figures of the prophet Zacharia and the Erythrean Sibyl on the left and the prophet Micah and the Cumean Sibyl on the right. The lower tier of the outer panels contains the single-figure, grisaille representations of Saint John the Baptist and Saint John the Evangelist. The saints are flanked by the portraits of the donors, Joos Vijd and his wife, Elizabeth Borluut. Aesthetically and iconographically, the exterior is coherent and consistent in its presentation of the mystery of the incarnation. When the altarpiece is opened, however, not only the sensuous richness of the Van Eycks' rendering of contrasting textures and sheens and the meticulous handling of detail and glowing color strongly contrast to the rather somber appearance of the outer panels, but the structure, scale, and the general conception of the interior's two tiers are incongruous. The five panels of the lower tier of the opened altarpiece, "The Adoration of the Lamb," present an almost panoramic scene of angels, groups of prophets, patriarchs, apostles, martyrs, and saints set against a continuous background of the meticulously rendered flowery meadows of paradise and the distant buildings of the New Jerusalem. The altarpiece's upper tier has three panels: God the Father, sometimes identified as Christ;[11] the Virgin Mary; and John the Baptist. The wing panels on the upper tier portray angels singing and playing musical instruments, large nude figures of Adam and Eve, and small grisaille figures that depict the story of Cain and Abel.

The three separate vertical pictures are superimposed upon a single oblong one, and in reverse of the usual altarpiece design, the scale of the figures in the upper panels is as colossal as that in the lower ones is small. Although the basic theme of the altarpiece is universal and unified in a chain of allusions and associations, its iconographic scheme remains controversial. Regardless of the specific interpretation of its iconography, there is general agreement that the main theme of the altarpiece is the Mystery of Redemption with its corollary theme of the Mystery of the Communion of Saints. These subjects are interwoven with allusions to historical events, to local and family circumstances, and to personal ambitions, and they reflect the aspirations and achievements of fifteenth-century Netherlandish art in much the same way that the ambiguities of Camus's *La Chute* reflect the feelings of twentieth-century Europe.

That Camus was aware of the altarpiece, and specifically of the missing panel of "The Just Judges," is easily documented by the text of *La Chute*. Undoubtedly the iconographic ambiguity of the polyptych attracted him as an artistic manifestation of the philosophic questioning and aesthetic experimentation that characterized Netherlandish art of the fifteenth century.[12] But the most apparent reason for Camus's fascination with the altarpiece was the prominent role allocated to John the Baptist in the Van Eycks' composition. John, here resplendent in his sumptuous green mantle worn over his camelhair shirt, is granted the unprecedented privilege of being enthroned on the side of God the Father.[13] In his left hand John holds a book in which "Comfort ye," the opening words of Isaiah's prophecy concerning the Baptist, are visible. The mouldings behind him are inscribed: "This is John the Baptist, greater than man, like unto the angels, the summation of the law, the propagator of the Gospels, the voice of the Apostles, the silence of the prophets, the lamp of the world, the witness of the Lord."[14]

These words are strikingly applicable to Jean-Baptiste's severe characterization of himself. He certainly perceives himself to be greater than those of the hypocritical bourgeois world he has rejected. If he is not "like unto the angels," it is only because his world of play actors has no merciful angels for him to emulate. The Christian God, being out of style, has been replaced by "Our Father who art provisionally here," and the essential law for survival has become "to cease being free and to obey, in repentance, a greater rogue than oneself" (136). He is the summation of the new law, the only law that has meaning in a world unable to accept responsibility for its freedom and unwilling to accuse and judge itself. He is "the end and the beginning" (118). He feels like God the Father as he "sits enthroned" among his "bad angels at the summit of the Dutch heaven" and watches as they ascend toward him, "as they issue from the fogs and the water, the multitude of the Last Judgment" (143).

It is not only in word, but also in physical appearance that the reader recognizes the Van Eycks' John the Baptist in Camus's Jean-Baptiste Clamence. A portrait, whether in words or in paint, always attempts to combine the seemingly contradictory qualities of individuality and totality. It aims to emphasize the uniqueness of its subject while at the same time showing the qualities that its subject shares with the rest of humanity. If the artist stresses only the subject's uniqueness, the subject is reduced to an infinity of qualities that are exclusively his or hers and is consequently separated from other human beings. On the other hand, if the artist stresses only the qualities the subject shares with others, that subject is reduced to such universal and basic characteristics that the subject ceases to be an individual in any sense of the word. This dilemma is recognized by almost all creative artists, and the greatest of them cannot be categorically described by either method. In the works of the Van Eycks and Camus, it is difficult to define their subjects in absolute psychological terms. We may know a great deal about the physical appearance of John the Baptist or of Jean-Baptiste Clamence, but the absence of the specific details that would give either of them an unqualifiable psychic or historical definition makes it impossible to grasp them as characters. Both artists, through a meticulous selection of details, present individuals who are obviously human, yet independent of place or time.[15] Like Jean-Baptiste Clamence, the Van Eycks and Camus "construct a portrait which is the image of all and of no one," and when the portrait is finished, it "becomes a mirror" (139–40) not only of ourselves but also of a world made to flicker and vibrate by the way it is seen. Perhaps these real, yet enigmatic artistic creations by the Van Eycks and Camus are best described by William James's comment upon his brother's method of constructing characters, "Their orbits," he writes, "come out of space and lay themselves for a short time alongside of ours, and then off they whirl into the unknown, leaving us with little more than an impression of their reality and a feeling of baffled curiosity as to the mystery of the beginning and end of their being."[16]

In Van Eycks' and Camus's works, the dual aspects of corporal reality and mystic unreality are set in a world that is difficult to delineate. The perspective or point of view used by a painter or an author can keep the viewer or reader at a distance from or intimately involved in the depicted scene. Since perspective presupposes the concept of an infinite space, but operates within a limited frame, it can emphasize the relative completeness or the absolute transcendence of what is presented or implied. In the Ghent Altarpiece, the architecture of the piece extends forward beyond the frame, around and over the spectator so that he or she stands within the scene. The viewer is visually carried into the painting in such a way that he or she, along with the characters portrayed, becomes a participant within the presented action. In the closed altarpiece, the Virgin's room, for example, is represented in the four panels of the middle register so that the frames form an open wall through which the viewer witnesses and participates in the event of the annunciation. The viewer feels included in the Virgin's room; yet the opened windows create a kind of blend between indoor and outdoor space, between the defined, limited space and the implied, universal space.

When the altarpiece is opened, the principal painting, "The Adoration of the Lamb," invites the viewer to join the great multitudes that surround the Lamb of God in the fields of paradise. Although the landscape of this panel, attributed to Hubert Van Eyck, suggests that he often worked from sketchbooks rather than from life, his perspective nonetheless penetrates beyond the limits of the immediate scene and presents a slice of infinity. Because the perspective is not completely unified and the landscape is somewhat artificial, the artist succeeds in creating another reality rather than an exact copy of nature.

Point of view and perspective are also key technical aspects of *La Chute*. Although the entire narrative is a monologue, and seemingly limited in point of view, Camus manipulates the story in such a way that once the reader has accepted Clamence's invitation to hear his confession, that confession becomes a vehicle that creates mirrored images and allusions that carry the reader outside the limits of the narrative's framework into infinite space. Since editorial commentary is ruled out, patterns of imagery and symbol become the controls for the reader's evaluation of details. Just as the viewer of the Van Eyck painting can identify portraits of such historical personages as Virgil and see them in relationship to the theology visually conveyed, so too in *La Chute* can the verbal allusion to Virgil evoke in the reader's mind the association among the worlds of Virgil and Dante and that of *La Chute*. This sense of infinity results from Camus's extension of the limits of time and space. The descriptive passages not only emanate directly from the narrative and intensify its dramatic action, but they also are infused with elements that carry the reader beyond the conscious level of thought into a realm that cannot be measured in clock time. The world of *La Chute* is not the world of twentieth-century Amsterdam, of first-century Palestine, or of fifteenth-century Ghent. It is all of these and greater than the summation of its individual parts.

Camus's invitation to examine the Ghent Altarpiece in relationship to *La Chute* comes from his specific reference to the left outermost panel of the altarpiece, "The Just Judges." Although the disappearance of this panel in 1934 provided the historical fact for Camus's reference to it, the choice obviously is intended to underline not only Clamence's former profession but also his misuse of that profession. Judges are traditionally those to whom earthly justice is entrusted; yet in medieval life, literature, and art, they represent a class of society that was often prayed for or against in Christian churches. Judges were frequently less than just, and their inclusion in the altarpiece does not result from their being an accepted category of saints but as the ideal representatives of a specific group of living dignitaries who hoped to be included with the Elect.[17]

Conclusion

Clamence also hoped to be admitted to the hierarchies of the Blessed when he assumed the role of judge-penitent. Through his adopted role of a modern prophet, he thought that he could lead us to admit our guilt and face the future without illusion. His every word begs for a structured outer law in which he would see himself reflected. But in Clamence's world there is no absolute law, no afterlife, no second coming, no dove of the Holy Spirit. The only doves that flutter overhead, whether they are the gulls near Marken or the flight that swirls amid the snowflakes, bring no clear answer. We, along with Clamence, remain doomed to live the sacrifice, incapable of filling the void left by the death of a patriarchal God, conscious of our fall, burdened with our fate, and unable to quench the anguish of our thirst. Yet the fall from the edenic life of innocence can also be seen as a fall into a state of heightened awareness, a state that may well awaken us from despair, cause us to take responsibility for our own lives with "all the weight of errors and greatness,"[18] and allow us to quench our thirst, freed from the desert of hopelessness. After all, according to Camus, "we shall choose in the reality of today or of yesterday what announces and serves the perfect city of the future."[19]

Great ideas come into the world as gently as doves. Perhaps then, if we listen attentively, we shall hear, amid the uproar of empires and nations, a faint flutter of wings, the gentle stirring of life and hope. Some will say that this hope lies in a nation; others, in a man. I believe rather that it is awakened, revived, nourished by millions of solitary individuals whose deeds and works every day negate frontiers and the crudest implications of history. As a result, there shines forth fleetingly the ever threatened truth that each and every man, on the foundation of his own sufferings and joys, builds for all. (208–9)

In *La Chute,* Camus has fictionalized the anguish of an age, and he offers no easy solution to this anguish. It is a truth as real and as powerful as the truth of absurdity and revolt, and in its own way it contributes powerfully to the understanding of modern men and women. Camus no longer wanted to see white and black, innocence and guilt, each concealing the other. He wished not only to place them side by side but to mingle them, to see *l'envers et l'endroit,* the exile and the kingdom as one. As Clamence warns us, his confession is addressed to the Sadducee in us, the part of each individual that clings to the status quo, to the letter of the law. In Camus's next major writing, *L'Exil et le royaume,* he sustains rather than negates our essentially enigmatic nature, and in the collection of short stories he portrays men and women who live with but do not torture themselves about the mixture of guilt and innocence, the multiple faces of us all.

Chapter Nine

The Earthly Kingdom

L'Exil et le royaume

L'Exil et le royaume (*Exile and the Kingdom*), Camus's last published creative work, contains some of his richest and most enigmatic writing. Published in 1957, the immediate reception of the collection reflected general disappointment. To a reading public whose image of Camus was that of a moralist and a spokesman for his generation, the volume was puzzling. He provided no answers to current philosophic and political questions, and he gave no direction to those who looked to him for guidance. The critical reception of the book reflected an equal degree of perplexity. The critics focused more upon the ideas that the six texts did not contain than they did upon Camus's extraordinary stylistic virtuosity. They tended to dismiss the short stories as experiments in style that Camus undertook in preparation for a new stage in his literary development. This early critical indifference has been corrected by more recent studies of the stories as artistic entities in themselves and as parts of a collection. Regardless of the textual ambiguities and the problematic relationship of the individual stories to each other and to the title of the volume, there is general agreement that in the six short stories Camus displays not only his ability to illuminate "the problems of the human conscience in our times," but also his poetic power to capture, assemble, and restore the "unique throbbing of life." In no other work since *Noces* has he so openly displayed his personal and inimitable stamp: his Algerian birth, his appreciation for the joys of the physical life, his understanding of human warmth and compassion, and his suffering from separation and loneliness.

These stories of men and women in search of an inner kingdom where they can forget their spiritual exile reveal little about the evolution of Camus's ideas, but they tell much about his longings for an Algeria that he could never forget. In Paris at this time he was not only in real exile from his native land; but by the force of circumstances in postwar France, he was also intellectually separated from his political beliefs and ideals. His private problems as an artist committed both to his art and his world are handled with superior deftness in these tales of men and women seen in differing moments of experience. A wife leaves her husband's bed to give herself completely to the desert night; a missionary, loving the savages who have tortured him, teaches the true meaning of intolerance; a melancholy workman fails to make contact with others and longs for the happier days of his lost youth; a French schoolmaster, in his desire to do good, suffers from a misunderstanding and is hated for a deed of love; an artist is caught between the demands of society and the pursuit of his art; and an engineer finds his place among others by learning to share their struggles. In each of these stories Camus concentrates upon the qualities and problems of an ordinary man or woman in a particular situation. Although these people suffer sharply from metaphysical fate and daily misery, they do not incarnate abstract ideas in the manner of Meursault, Rieux, or Clamence. They are middle-aged members of ordinary humanity who neither withdraw from the facts of life nor sacrifice themselves to them. Without ever quite forgetting their own individuality, they are able to join others by sharing their struggles. The entire human being is found again in the fruits and flowers of the land, in the union of land and sea, in the coming together of two strong young bodies, in the inundation of the whole being with the loveliness of earth, and in the individual's power to endure. Each character's discovery of the self and its relationship to others is limited by time. In all the stories, narrated from the characters' points-of-view, the reader is aware that the related events are highlighted moments in the individuals' lives and that these same individuals will again return to exile. They have glimpsed, but not possessed, the kingdom.

The Central Theme

The unity of the collection is conveyed by Camus's emphasis on the theme of separation that all of the stories reflect, but at the same time each piece remains a separate work of art. More than any other single device, it is the stylistic excellence and the diversity of expression that Camus employs as he moves from one story to another that sets the entire volume apart and makes it unique. The descriptive language of "La Femme adultère" ("The Adulterous Woman") and "La Pierre qui pousse" ("The Growing Stone"); the stream-of-consciousness technique of "Le Renégat" ("The Renegade"); the humor and irony of "Jonas" ("The Artist at Work"); the directness of "Les Muets" ("The Silent Men") and "L'Hôte" ("The Guest") provide a showcase for Camus's artistic virtuosity. From his combination of an active creative power with a skilled mastery of language, characters emerge that "by some miracle of art . . . continue to live, while ceasing to be mortal (*The Rebel*, 226).

Camus's Theory of Art

The discussion of style in *L'Homme révolté* helps the reader to understand Camus's intentions in *L'Exil et le royaume*. In *L'Homme révolté*, Camus develops his theory of art in general with emphasis upon the art of the novel. Although Camus labels *L'Etranger* and *La Chute* as "récits" and *La Peste* as a "chronique," all of his works clearly illustrate the stylization of reality that he thought characteristic of the greatest art. In *L'Homme révolté*, he argues that all artists in one way or another revolt against the natural formlessness of life and reconstruct the world according to their own plan. By extracting from natural disorder a unity that is more satisfying to the mind and the heart, the artist restores form to the general confusion of reality. The artist's arrangement and selection of details from reality in no way implies a failure to understand and to acknowledge the fact of reality, for to ignore it would result in a mediocre effort to escape it rather than to clarify and order it. Quite the opposite of rejecting the real world, the world of art is the same world of suffering, illusion, and love that we know. This world is neither more beautiful nor more enlightening than ours, and the heroes speak our language and have our weaknesses and strengths. But the artist, through an exercise of selectivity, creates out of the chaotic world known to us a world that is peopled by men and women who complete things that we in the real world can never complete. The events that make up our lives are without pattern, and it is the rare individual who can give life the fixed and irredeemable quality he or she desires. But through the controlling hand of the artist, the fictional character is allowed to pursue his or her destiny without the interruptions that a real situation imposes. According to Camus, it is this factor of completion that gives art its meaning and its appeal. Although we fully realize that the worlds of fictional characters are not ours, we can identify with them; and because of the order that their lives contain, we can fulfill our aesthetic need for a unified world. Thus, the imaginary world that the artist creates from the rectification of the actual world surpasses our world, for it gives us the "alleviating form and limits" that we vainly pursue in our own lives.

Camus thought that within this sealed world created by the artist "man can reign and have knowledge at last" (255). Through the artist's isolation of subject matter in time and space, he or she unifies and reconstructs the world according to a preconceived plan and can "stylize and imprison one significant expression" in order to illuminate one aspect of the "infinite variety of human attitudes" (256). Although the world in all its manifestations is valid territory for artistic exploration, in the creation of the imaginary world, the artist cannot totally reject reality, for unity is not communicable in the purely imaginable. The true artist uses reality with "all its warmth and its blood" and adds something that transfigures it. "This correction which the artist imposes by his language and by a redistribution of elements derived from reality, is called style and gives the recreated universe its unity and its boundaries" (269).

Camus's created universe indicates that the general movement of his artistic attitude has been toward aesthetic unity. In his search for human destiny, he has consistently refused the world as he found it and sought to create a unified world that could be understood. Through his description of a closed universe, he has allowed all his characters, from Meursault through Rieux to Clamence, the luxury of attempting to create a substitute universe that possesses the unity they demand. They neither renounce nor reject the actual world, but they refuse the disorder they find in it and fabricate order and unity out of the chaos that surrounds them.

Although this aspect of Camus's art is consistent, there is a distinguishable philosophic difference between his early and his later writings. The juxtaposition of the individual's need for unity and the world's disunity is the same in the absurd writings and works following the development of Camus's philosophy of limits. In the absurd experiment, however, Camus felt no compulsion to construct a world of order and value, for any devised system of unity was condemned to die along with its creator. In the philosophy of limits, however, the individual is called upon to recreate the world in spite of death, for it is only through a recognition of the individual's power to effect a positive change in the values of the world that any hope for happiness exists. In simple terminology, it is Sisyphus's recognition that he is not alone in an indifferent universe.

These ideas are significant not only to the narrative art of *L'Exil et le royaume,* but also to an understanding of the characters' motivations. In their search for an earthly kingdom, they are all aware of their positions in the world. Each of the stories focuses on a given person in that particular moment in which he or she is searching for value in a world of constant change and endless contradiction. In a sense they all know that they will never achieve final triumph in their struggle with the world; but they also know that for their lives to have any meaning, they must follow the only course open to them and create their own values within the limits imposed by their human nature. They echo Camus's statement in *L'Homme révolté* that, "on my self alone rests the common dignity which I cannot allow to be debased either in myself or others."

"La Femme adultère"

"La Femme adultère" is the first story of the collection and the only one to have a woman as its central figure. Janine, the middle-aged protagonist, accompanies her husband on a business trip among the villages of southern Algeria. The trip is at first nothing more than another in a series of such trips that she had made out of duty; but once in the vastness and silence of the desert, she is strangely attracted to the nomadic tribesmen who "since the beginning of time . . . had been ceaselessly trudging, possessing nothing but serving no one, poverty-stricken but free lords of a strange kingdom".[1] Contemplating her own life, its lost youth, her cheated heart, she identifies the nomadic kingdom as her own: a kingdom that had been promised to her from all time. The chain of habit and boredom that was her life up to this time gradually dissolves as she finds in her own heart "something of which, though it had always been lacking, she had never been aware of until now" (23). She realizes in this vast expanse of territory, where life is suspended and time stands still, that she must instantly seize this "something" or never again know its meaning.

That evening she leaves her sterile marriage bed to escape into the night and to recapture the lost kingdom of her youth. In the rapturous yielding of her body to the universe, she consummates her adultery with the forces of nature. In an emotionally charged passage, Camus describes Janine's complete surrender of her body to the "sky in movement," as she identifies herself with the core of her being. She momentarily forgets "the cold, the dead weight of others, the craziness or stuffiness of life, the long anguish of living and dying." She takes the sky unto herself and sated, she falls onto the cold earth (32–33). Much later she returns to her marriage bed, her exile. For only a brief moment, she was able to escape the coldness and loneliness of her life and be totally at one with the mystery and the splendor of the universe.

In this story, along with the others of the collection, the central event is neither analyzed nor agonized over. In a poetic, rather than a political or philosophic sense, these tales reflect Camus's statement in *L'Homme révolté* that "real generosity towards the future lies in giving all to the present" (271). The heroism of these characters lies in their ability to feel and act upon situations with a grandeur that Camus has consistently found to be an essential aspect of life. Through their actions he suggests the complexities of life more than he proposes answers to them or gives a roadmap to the earthly kingdom. They search for purity, for rest, for home, but they know that their search cannot ever be completed, that their escape from exile is only temporary.

"Le Renégat"

"Le Renégat," the second story of the collection, centers on the misdirection of the will to self-expression. The protagonist of this story, significantly subtitled "Un Esprit confus" ("A Confused Man"), is a French missionary who has taken upon himself the impossible task of converting a particularly barbarous African tribe. As the story develops, we discover that not only is he physically removed from his native environment, but more significantly he is an exile from the true meanings of the Christianity he professes to teach. His religion has never been more than a means for him to settle his account with his "pig of a father," his teachers, "the whole of lousy Europe." He longed for nothing more than the power his religion gave him to make people kneel down, to force them to capitulate, to be converted, and "the blinder, the crueler he [the convert] is, the more he's sure of himself, mired in his own conviction, the more his consent establishes the royalty of whoever brought about his collapse" (39). To the missionary truth is heavy and thick, and good is an idle dream. "Only evil is present, down with Europe, reason, honor, and the cross" (54).

In this nightmarish monologue, told in a series of flashbacks, Camus is certainly experimenting with the stream-of-consciousness technique popularized in France by the writings of Faulkner;[2] however, more significant than the stylistic experiment is the repetition of one of the central themes of the entire collection of short stories. Camus is once again saying that inherent goodness can be easily misdirected by chance. By a misunderstanding of meaning, by the chance of being born "bright but . . . pigheaded" (35), one can be totally misguided. Because of reasons beyond his control, the missionary mistook his will to power for charity. He left the monastery convinced that he could convert the barbarous tribes to his religion. It is, however, he who is converted, and the overwhelming failure of his mission results in his imprisonment and the eventual transfer of the unthinking allegiance he had to Christ to a blind worship of the savages' idol. An insoluble conflict results from the clash of two equally wrong commitments. Both the extremes of Christianity and of paganism are impossible to follow. In either case the individual is exiled from the human kingdom. To underline the need for tolerance in order to live within the earthly realm, the true nature of tolerance and humility is revealed to the missionary at the moment of his death: "Cast off that hate-ridden face, be good now, we were mistaken, we'll begin all over again, we'll rebuild the city of mercy, I want to go home" (61).

In some ways reminiscent of Cottard in *La Peste,* this young missionary also cannot know the kingdom of "fraternal man." The anguish, torture, and pain inflicted upon Cottard and this central figure are caused by an ill-defined aspect of existence that Camus repeatedly refuses to make explicit, but is nonetheless a powerful negative component of his universe. It is related to and recalls the theme of misunderstanding, but in this story the negative originates from two forces within rather than outside the individual. "Le Renégat" restates the thesis of *La Chute* that good and evil are equally inherent in everyone, and it is a question of chance as to which will dominate. The missionary, like Clamence, embodies an attitude that is examined in all its consequences. Both men have experienced the absurdity of the world, and they have lost their beliefs in human dignity. They react to their exiles with unheard cries of despair—a despair that can only be alleviated by a freer life and an unattainable transcendence of life's imposed and inescapable limits.

"Les Muets"

On a less individual level and certainly on a more melancholy and personal one, "Les Muets" reiterates the collection's prevalent concern with misunderstanding and lack of communication. This story, unlike the first two, does not only involve the relationship of one individual to the universe; but in a realistic, simple, and direct way, it also presents the complex problems of people out of tune with others and with their times. The "silence" of the title underscores the only way these people have to express the anger, helplessness, fear, and anxiety they suffer because of their exile.

On the surface, "Les Muets" is a story of the inevitable changes brought about by an evolving economy. These men, returning to work after twenty days of unsuccessful striking, are helplessly caught between two equally right forces. Their trade of cooperage was threatened by the building of tankers and tank trucks and simply was not thriving. On the one hand, the cooper could not change his trade, "you don't change trades when you've gone to the trouble of learning one" (65); while on the other hand, the only way the employer could maintain a necessary margin of profit was to block wages. Characteristic of most of Camus's conflicts, there is no obvious solution to the dilemma. Neither the men nor the boss is either totally right or wrong. The men were forced to return to work because of "wives sad at home" (67) or their own discouragement, but they resented the fact that their mouths had been closed; and the anger and helplessness hurt so much that they could not even cry out in protest. "They were men, after all" (78). Out of frustration and in order to give some expression to their dissatisfaction, they formed a coalition of silence against their employer's plea to "try to work together" (76).

The predicament that Camus presents is particularly intense in his native Algeria, and he treats it compassionately and sympathetically. The kingdom that all these men long for is the realm of love and understanding, and the exile that they suffer is their exclusion from the fraternal universe. The only union they eventually find is in family affection, but even here they are incapable of communication and remain silent. Yet, optimistically, Camus implies that in the unspoken solidarity that the men experience through their reactions to the illness of their employer's daughter, in their renewed contact with the twilight beauty of the earth and sea around them, and in their love for their wives and families, they are at least momentarily reintegrated into the earthly kingdom.

It is clear from the first three stories of the collection that most of Camus's characters suffer from the anxiety of having to decide their relationship to themselves and to others. They encounter situations that are foreign to them, that test them by taking them out of their routinely organized existences, and that force them to decide between "exile" and "kingdom." If the examples Camus uses seem marginal to ordinary experience and at times inexplicable, it must be remembered that these stories continue his exploration of the difficulties that beset the exile in the lonely and independent effort to be a man or woman— an attempt that is, as Tarrou said in *La Peste,* more ambitious than to be a saint. And it must also be remembered that the absurd truth of life is that only in exile can the faint glimmerings of the kingdom be seen and enjoyed.

"L'Hôte"

In "L'Hôte," a story of tragic misunderstanding, a schoolteacher in North Africa is given the task of delivering to the authorities an Arab accused of killing his cousin in a quarrel over grain. By every means available to him, Daru, the teacher, attempts to give the Arab his freedom. He conveys his understanding of and sympathy for him by feeding and looking after him. He refuses to bind him and is disappointed when he does not attempt to escape during the night. The next morning Daru takes his charge to a point where two paths lead in divergent directions. Turning him toward the road that leads to the desert and to freedom, and away from the road toward town, judgment, and prison, Daru leaves the Arab to make his own decision. As Daru returns toward the schoolhouse, he looks back and sees the Arab "slowly walking along the road to prison" (109).

As a schoolteacher, Daru has no authority to free the Arab from the murder charge. At the same time, however, as a human being he cannot send him to imprisonment and death. By allowing the Arab to choose between the two roads, Daru fulfills his responsibility as a human being by not infringing on the Arab's right to decide the direction his life is to take. The fact that the Arab does not understand Daru's actions is insignificant. Daru has done what he believes is right by remaining true to the laws of humanity rather than those of society.

When the schoolmaster returns to his classroom, he finds written in clumsily chalked-up words, "You handed over our brother. You will pay for this" (109). This threat of an invisible witness and this complete misunderstanding of his intended generosity make Daru aware that "in this vast landscape he had loved so much, he was alone" (109). His helplessness and frustration, resulting from his inability to communicate the meaning of his actions to the Arab, poignantly illustrate the position of the person who refrains from accepting the dogmatic pronouncements of either political parties or systematic ideologies. Daru is unable to ally himself with either the French administration or the Arab rebel movement. The only thing that he can be certain of is that the "rotten spite . . . tireless hates . . . blood lusts" (93) have solved nothing in the past and are unlikely to better future social, economic, and political conditions. Although Daru's actions result in the seemingly negative and meaningless facts that he offended a policeman, that the Arab chose punishment over freedom, that he himself is now exposed to an unjustifiable reprisal, he has maintained his dignity as a man who believes that "it's worth more to be wrong without killing anyone and in allowing others to talk, than to be right in the midst of silence and charnel houses" (*Actuelles I*, 267).

There is no comfortable solution for the characters caught in Camus's paradox of exile and kingdom. He offers none, for like many twentieth-century authors, he wants his readers to confront the situations he describes and decipher a meaning that extends beyond the specific problem he presents. His characters are not individualized, for they must embody general or universal human characteristics; yet they simultaneously must all act as individuals who are able to make decisions, to go beyond routine existence, and to reach the highest and most difficult victory over absurdity. Whether they are right or wrong, whether they reach the kingdom or not, is not the issue. They choose, they act, and they accept responsibility. In that way they are heroic. Yet the paradox persists. The meaning they find results in no long-term solution, and they each return to a life of isolation and loneliness that in many ways is more unbearable than what they endured before they glimpsed the kingdom.

"Jonas"

In "Jonas, ou l'artiste au travail," Camus complicates the paradox by allowing Jonas to destroy his own integrity through futile attempts to enter the lives of everyone he knows. In spite of its underlying serious meaning, "Jonas" is the wittiest and most amusing of Camus's writings. The story involves a Parisian painter of modest talent who trusted in his "star" to bring him fame and good fortune. After he was discovered by an art dealer, he was immediately beset by fame and its consequent frustrations. As he became better known, new friends arrived in scores to invade his already crowded apartment and to while away his afternoons "begging Jonas to go on working . . . for they . . . knew the value of an artist's time" (125). It soon became impossible for Jonas to paint at all. He was constantly surrounded by disciples who "explained to him at length what he had painted and why," and in this way "Jonas discovered in his work many intentions that rather surprised him, and a host of things he hadn't put there" (127). Gradually Jonas completely lost his natural approach to his art and assumed the pose his admirers expected. As time passed he painted less and less, but ironically enough, "the less he worked, the more his reputation grew" (131). The more his name appeared in print, the more often he was asked to take part "in exposing most revolting injustices" (133). The more his apartment became invaded by people who had respect for him but did not know or care about his work, the less he was the artist they professed to praise. Amid the confusion caused by the visitors, disciples, and critics jammed into a flat that was already too small for his wife and three children, Jonas finally was totally absorbed in activities other than creative. His inspiration left him at the height of his fame. When he was asked to pose for a portrait of the artist at work, he no longer had either the time or the spirit to paint.

Frantically searching for somewhere peaceful to paint, Jonas, in a series of bizarre moves, abandons his studio for the bedroom, the bedroom for the corridor, the corridor for the shower, the shower for the kitchen. But his star began to fail him, and now no matter where he was "he would think of painting, of his vocation, instead of painting" (144). In desperation he turns to cognac and other women and is temporarily consoled with the illusion of creativity and vitality. At times it even seems to him that his old strength is returning; and one day, encouraged by one of his female friends, he returns home to begin again. He constructs a kind of loft in a high corner of his flat and retreats there to meditate and "discover what he had not yet clearly understood although he had always known it and had always painted as if he knew it. He had to grasp at last that secret which was not merely the secret of art, as he could now see" (153). After many days of retreat, during which time he sees only his friend Radeau and eats practically nothing, he falls ill. Radeau took the canvas on which Jonas had been working and found written "in very small letters a word that could be made out, but without any certainty as to whether it should be read *solitary* or *solidary*" (158). In his flight from others, Jonas finally confronts his own consciousness, and through this confrontation he realizes the balance he must strike between his involvement with and his distance from others. His salvation lies in an earthly kingdom that will allow him the inner freedom he must have to create.

Based upon Camus's personal experiences, and beyond its satirical and humorous elements, the story reflects Camus's concern about the artist's role in society. In his notebooks and in several of his essays and lectures, he frequently tried to come to some sort of understanding of his own commitment to art. In an interview with Jean Bloch-Michel, Camus underscored the position of the contemporary writer who is forced to choose between engagement and total isolation:

That's how it is with the artist of our age: he runs the risk, if he stays in his ivory tower, of cutting himself off from reality, or, if he gallops forever around the political arena, of drying up. The ticklish paths of true art lie somewhere between the two. It seems to me that the writer should not ignore the conflicts of his time, and that he should take part in them when he knows that he can. But he should also keep, or from time to time recover, a definite perspective towards our history. Every work presupposes some factual content to which a creator has given shape. Though the artist should share in the misfortunes of his age, he must also try to stand off a bit to contemplate and formalize what he sees. This eternal return, this tension which can be, frankly, a dangerous game at times, is the burden of the artist today. Perhaps this means that, in short order, there will no longer be any artists. But maybe not. It is a question of time, of energy, of freedom, and also of chance.[3]

The above passage clearly expresses Camus's conviction that it is impossible to dictate to artists that they must be engaged with the same preoccupations as other people. This idea is central in the story of Jonas. According to Camus, artists are most atune to the times when they are most solitary, and only in this way can they find the necessary energy to create great art and through their creations make "the human visage more admirable and richer."

"La Pierre qui pousse"

It is not to the artist, but to life as an art, that Camus turns in the final story of *L'Exil et le royaume*. In many ways "La Pierre qui pousse" is not only the most compelling story of the collection, but it also presents a dramatic statement of and provides a temporary solution to many of the problems that run through Camus's work from the time of his first essays. In all his writings—never negating his original premise that God does not exist—he continually searches for some kind of victory over absurdity. Sometimes he judges and criticizes what he finds in the world about him; sometimes he analyzes his own actions and passions; but the fundamental question that runs throughout his work remains the same. He consistently and directly asks for a clear and concise definition of what it means to lead a life as a man or woman born in an absurd universe.

"La Pierre qui pousse" gives one possible answer to this question. The protagonist, a French engineer, left his native Europe to build a dam in the small Brazilian town of Iguape. His arrival at the village coincides with an annual religious festival. The natives regard d'Arrast, the engineer, as an outsider, and he is, in fact, an outsider in many ways. He not only comes from another continent with a contrasting culture, but he also is a Roman Catholic who, according to his own admission, never found his "place" within the church. Perhaps even more striking than these facts is that the "shame and wrath" of his self-inflicted exile is emphasized by his questionable passport and by his attempted escape from his past guilt. He tells the cook, "Someone was about to die through my fault" (187).

In this remote village, d'Arrast enters into no real contact with others until on the day before the festival when a village cook tells him about a vow he made many years ago. He was in imminent danger of drowning and promised Jesus that if He saved him he would carry a hundred-pound stone on his head on the day of His procession. "You don't have to believe me," he told d'Arrast, "but the waters became calm and my heart too. I swam slowly, I was happy, and I reached the shore. Tomorrow I'll keep my promise" (183). Without really knowing why, other than for the simple reason that "he looked at the handsome frank face smiling trustingly at him, its dark skin gleaming with health and vitality" (185), d'Arrast promises the cook to help him keep his pledge. This is d'Arrast's first successful attempt toward communication with the villagers, but the gesture does not immediately end his isolation. That evening during the celebration in honor of Saint George, d'Arrast observes the natives' frenzied singing and dancing and becomes entranced by the violent beating of the drums, the heat, the dust, the smoke, and the smell of bodies; but he remains an outsider and is unable to forget himself totally and join the natives' sacrifice of their individuality. He is brutally reminded of the fact that he is an alien when the cook tells him, "They are going to dance all night long, but they don't want you to stay now" (197).

D'Arrast does not establish an emotionally satisfying contact with these people until the day of the holy procession. As he has done in the past, the cook takes up his burden and joins the procession, but it soon is obvious that his strength is not sufficient for the task he has undertaken. He falters, sweats, strains, and finally collapses in an agony of body and spirit. D'Arrast leaps to his side, lifts the stone to his own head, and proceeds toward the church. He had already gone beyond the center of the church square when "without knowing why, he veered off to the left and turned away from the church" (210). He reaches the cook's hovel, his breath beginning to fail, his arms trembling under the stone, and brusquely hurls the stone "onto the still glowing fire in the center of the room" (212). There "he felt rising within him a surge of obscure and panting joy that he was powerless to name" (212), and he acclaims "a fresh beginning in life." Through his actions d'Arrast declares his brotherhood with those who labor and are heavy laden. That his actions are understood is made clear by the natives' invitation to "sit down with us" (213). No longer a stranger, d'Arrast has conquered his separation and loneliness and has found a place where he belongs.

It is characteristic of Camus's thought that in this story he transfers the shrine from the church to the hearth of a man who has the courage to keep a promise freely made. Never conceiving himself to be an abstract philosopher, Camus's consistent concern has been to communicate an individual experience that is illuminated and universalized through his art. Rather than depending on abstractions to convey his ideas, Camus relied in his fiction on frequently unresolved tensions to create his impact. In this final story, d'Arrast has found his place in the community of Iquape, but there is no implied guarantee that his happiness will endure. It matters little if it does not. The important thing is that he has found meaning to his life through his complete involvement in the experiences and actions of others. He has discovered a brotherhood among all of those who devote their lives unselfishly to others.

Evaluation

In many ways this collection of short stories is both a beginning and an end. At least momentarily Camus was willing to turn away from philosophic writing and to concentrate on human beings in actual situations. Many critics have pointed out that these stories were partially experiments in style for the projected novel, *Le Premier Homme*. And as the reader moves from one story to the next, he or she cannot help but be aware of the collection's virtuoso display of technical variety. Camus proves over and over again that his power to evoke place and atmosphere is as great as his ability to show the duality of body and spirit. Not only do his characters have individual mannerisms that silently reveal their personalities, but the features of the scenes in which they move also create an atmosphere that reflects the stories' significance.

The inconclusive nature of some of the stories in the collection invites the reader to search for a switch in Camus's philosophic position that would bridge the gap between his completed Promethean cycle and his projected cycle of Nemesis. But rather than any dramatic change in Camus's thought processes, the collection reiterates his ongoing quest for the ever illusive midpoint between the extremities of life, between *l'envers et l'endroit* and *l'exil et le royaume*. The present and the past collide in *L'Exil et le royaume*. The characters of these stories, although older and less optimistic than Meursault or Caligula, share their realization of how difficult, if not impossible, it is to attain and sustain a reconciliation with nature; yet they, like all of Camus's characters, are free to choose and to act in their quest to find meaning in a world without a god or any other form of an absolute. The meaning they discover may be fleeting, but it derives from their recognition of and revolt against the solitude they suffer in an indifferent universe. They are strangers in a foreign environment who discover one or two moments that end their exile and give them a glimpse of the kingdom.

Conclusion

Camus's Position in Twentieth-Century Letters

Late in the twentieth century, many years since Camus's fatal accident, it remains difficult to predict the position he will occupy in literary history. The rapidity of change in every aspect of living has made even the most percipient of us hesitant to judge anything today without knowing tomorrow. The unknown of the future can be an extremely potent force. There is also a second reason that makes it difficult to categorize Camus's future reputation. Without fully trusting the time-worn truism that greater objectivity can be obtained when a writer's work is temporally removed from the critic, I find myself calling on that truism in this particular situation. One has only to think of Heidegger, Alfred North Whitehead, C.G. Jung, Faulkner, Thomas Mann, Rainer Maria Rilke, Tennessee Williams, Malraux, Graham Greene, Robert Frost, T. S. Eliot, Martin Buber, Jaspers, Sartre, Kafka, Marcel Proust, Ernest Hemingway—to name some of the outstanding poets, novelists, philosophers, and playwrights of the century, and the immediate response to such a random list is not one of amazement over the unquestionable greatness of these men, but it is rather one of amazement over the fact that the list does not include such established people as Saul Bellow, Günter Grass, Arnold Toynbee, Paul Tillich, Brecht, and so forth, and so forth. It becomes a kind of literary game to pick and choose the favorite players of the moment. Can any one of us with completely objective assurance say that Camus is greater than Faulkner but less great than Mann, or Mann greater than Faulkner but not so great as Camus? I think that the absurdity of the game is obvious.

So the task of placing Camus in his exact position is not an easy one. There is no doubt that his writings fit into the mainstream of twentieth-century thought. He, like many of the other writers mentioned, reflects the problematic existence that people in the Western world have been forced to endure following the calamities of the century. He, again as do most of these artists, tries to come to terms with himself and his world and to discover new values that will take the place of traditional theological and humanistic ones. What he creates to substitute for a belief in God or a belief in social and scientific progress also is not totally his. His literary and philosophic indebtedness is wide-reaching, and he reflects the influence of his exposure to the Greek classics, to the French writings of Madame de Lafayette, Gide, Proust, Malraux, and Henri de Montherlant, to the Czechoslovakian Kafka, the Russians Dostoevski and Tolstoy, to the theatrical master-pieces of Molière, Shakespeare, Lope de Vega, to the Americans Mel-ville, Hemingway, and Faulkner. This impressive list does not actually distinguish Camus from many writers of our century. As a matter of fact, the list itself hardly distinguishes him from any well-educated person today. But the thought and art that he sought to emulate from these writers does bear his particular stamp. These authors stimulated his mind and encouraged him to develop the unique quality that sets him apart from all of the writers of this time.

Camus's Intellectual Odyssey

In Camus's wrestling with the human condition, as we proceed from one work to the next, there is ever present a strong voice that is speaking for itself, in humility and trust, to an audience that has undergone experiences parallel to his own. His strong voice tells his audience that it need not suffer alone. Although the world may remain somewhat incomprehensible, events may happen that are inexplicable; yet he tells us that we are free to search for a unifying principle in our lives, that if we do inquire into the problems of existence, we can derive something out of life other than eating, drinking, sleeping, dressing, and undressing. It is Camus's insistence that we constantly reach upward—not to an unknown heaven—but to a better understanding of the present moment that provides his unique contribution to modern thought. His allegiance to the values of individual lives, of moderation, and of nature gives his writing a positive character and distinguishes it from much contemporary writing, which offers us nothing other than negative awareness. He tells us that the world is absurd, but that there are reasons to want to go on living; and it is from this desire to live that we can begin to build and create a universe that approaches what we would like it to be. It is the image of Sisyphus that comes to mind here; and although it may be difficult to imagine Sisyphus happy, it is not impossible to grant Sisyphus's triumph over despair. Camus finds mean-ing in Sisyphus's and our own struggle to create meaning in an absurd world, and it is this faint glimmer of hope that he holds before us that makes his voice more meaningful than that of many others.

He is a man of his age. His writings not only reflect the conflicts, the violence, and the lack of communication that are a part of our everyday world, but they also reveal his private concern with the far-reaching problems of this century. As we follow his intellectual odyssey from the recognition of absurdity through his complex concept of revolt, we are made increasingly aware of the conflicting demands of modern life. What we may have subconsciously perceived as the reasons for our instability are made unquestionably clear through his projection of our own frustrations into the central characters of his imaginative writings. There is no doubt that these heroes reflect the spirit and the pulse of contemporary life. Like them we tend to live from day to day with little sense of an enduring purpose in life, and also like them we try to work out for ourselves a satisfying philosophy to give life some direction and meaning. They, as we, have inherited the uncertainties of our age. It is no longer possible to assume the moral and religious convictions our ancestors took for granted. The ultimate meaning they found in religious or humanistic terms has been weakened by the disturbing facts of the past. The poet W. H. Auden said that "aloneness is man's real condition," and Camus echoes his voice; but unlike most voices of this century, Camus is not willing to stop there. Once he subscribes to the state of aloneness, he sets out to create new values that will again give life meaning and men and women responsible roles in the universe.

Through his art Camus explores an experience that gives an exact image of men and women within the intellectual climate of the twentieth century. He endows his characters with attitudes, feelings, and experiences latent among all of us, and he makes us aware of our anxieties, isolation, and anonymity. He forces us to realize that scientific and technological advancement, and the consequent material comforts, actually have nothing to do with happiness. He leads us to discover that rather than progressing, we are in the midst of the greatest decline experienced by any civilization. Instead of feeling more at home in the world through the conquests of science, we find ourselves alone and frightened in an indifferent universe. He diagnoses the characteristics of our age and relives in art the fundamental problems of life common to all of us. What emerges is not only a communication of personal experience, but also a valid work of art concerned with concrete problems in today's world.

As Camus leads his readers from *L'Envers et l'endroit* to *L'Exil et le royaume*, he gradually evolves a philosophy that bears his particular seal. From the cosmic pessimism that characterizes *Le Mythe de Sisyphe* to the philosophy of revolt most clearly developed in *L'Homme révolté*, he constantly corrects, without ever completely negating, his original position. He begins his absurd experiment with *L'Etranger* and *Le Mythe de Sisyphe*. In their denunciation of hope and their refusal of any metaphysical comfort, these books artistically reflect Camus's provisional attitude toward the contradiction between the longing for immortality and the inevitability of death. As we have seen, his aim from the beginning was only to examine and not to proffer the philosophy of the absurd. From his search for truth in a world that offers no hope and no illusions, he found that as men and women we have the right to challenge the world at every moment, to be passionately aware of every experience, and to be conscious of our freedom to exhaust everything that is given. The next step in Camus's experiment was to test these concepts in order to discover whether or not human dignity could persist in a world that granted each individual unlimited freedom. In the characterization of Meursault, Camus had already implied that one could not live happily or productively if all events were thought to be equal, but it is in the dramas of *Le Malentendu* and *Caligula* that the specific idea of freedom is pushed to its limits. The mad emperor Caligula's attempt to transform the world by exercising his unbound freedom is more spectacular than that of Jan in *Le Malentendu*, but both men are defeated by a very simple truth that they failed to recognize. There is a standard of values inherent in human nature that, as Cherea says, finds certain actions "more beautiful than others." At this juncture in the development of his thought, Camus imposes a limit upon human freedom. All actions are not equivalent and a judgment of them can be made without invoking sources beyond human experience. He is increasingly aware of the relationship between individual happiness and the attitude and conduct of others; and he clearly sees that a world void of a belief in moral principles, in which the individual is free to act in accordance with his or her own desires, could lead to a total disregard for the life and the welfare of others. He now adds to the original concept of absurdity the idea of limits. Complete freedom does not exist.

In Camus's early writings the idea of limits was implicit in *L'Etranger* and clearly stated in *Caligula*. At this early date Camus was aware that the absurdity of the world was a fact that had to be accepted, but he was equally aware of another fact. He realized that although the world could not be altered, those who suffer from its absurdity could create a life of meaning, unity, and value. This concept runs throughout all of Camus's writing, but it is only clearly defined in the works following *Caligula*. No one can doubt that it is the philosophy of revolt that dominates his thinking from that time until his death. He abandons the futile problem of death in an absurd world and focuses upon the problem of life. He accepts the world as it is, but he is not willing to accept men and women as they are. We may never be able to defeat the injustice of the universe, but we can defeat the injustice of others. The world is absurd because that is the nature of the universe, but history need not be absurd, for it is controlled by our actions. The oppression we suffer because of false ideas and ideologies can be eliminated, and it is to the specific condemnation of human error that Camus turns his attention after *Caligula*. His rebellion is directed against those people and institutions that refuse to respect the value of human nature and to accept the clearly defined limits of human behavior. It is with *La Peste* that Camus switches his emphasis from the intellectual problems of the universe to the more personal problems of the individual. Here he investigates the possibility of finding a series of values not only to satisfy the individual but also to be commended to others on universal grounds. He finds these values in the basic dignity and inherent worth of each individual human life. Camus himself remarked that *La Peste* indicated a change from "an attitude of solitary revolt to the recognition of a community whose struggles all must share." And in the same way that the absurd experiment was carried to its extreme in the two earlier dramas, *Le Malentendu* and *Caligula,* the idea of revolt and limits is now further analyzed in *L'Etat de siège* and *Les Justes*. It is in these plays that he searches for the humanitarian spirit that restores the value of human life. The individual is now placed in the enviable position of being able to realize high human ideals through the exercise of moral consciousness.

If we think back to the theory expressed in *Le Mythe de Sisyphe* and contrast it to the ideas expressed in *L'Homme révolté*, the distance that separates the literature of the absurd from the literature of revolt becomes increasingly clear. In *Le Mythe de Sisyphe*, Camus stated that "for the absurd man, it is no longer a question of explaining or resolving, but of feeling and describing. All begins with a clear-visioned indifference. To describe: this is the ultimate ambition of absurd thinking" (131). By contrast, in the literature of revolt no one can afford to be an indifferent stranger. We live in the same absurd world, bereft of all metaphysical aid. But rather than being satisfied to describe that world, Camus now insists that we must fashion a world of unity and value. He realized that in a completely absurd world the only values that could be established would be created from an extremely personal point of view and would only be tenable in a particular historical epoch. The solitary reflections of a Sisyphus must therefore give way to the forceful actions of a Prometheus. Through our own "sweat and blood" we must shape values and formulate attitudes that will do justice to the human condition. There is no room for apathy and resignation. We must act and through actions establish an order that carries us beyond negation to the affirmation of life.

It is at this point that the experiment should be completed. The original premise has been investigated by the essayist and clarified by the novelist and playwright. The individual has grappled with the forces that menace freedom, and by the strength of intelligence and sympathy, has emerged victoriously. Through an intense and honest inquiry into the nature of men and women and the meaning of the universe, Camus has molded a formless mass into a coherent whole. The world may still deny the individual a rightful place, but the conscious person can regain the lost kingdom by constantly using intelligence to oppose, control, and destroy the social patterns that oppress. The experiment should have ended, but it did not.

Not satisfied with the results of his investigation of the absurd and the philosophy of revolt, Camus now begins his analysis of the other side of the coin. His portrayal of Clamence in *La Chute* as a man who not only knows himself to be self-centered, dishonest, and hypocritical but as one who also seeks to prove to others that they are exactly like him injects a measure of pessimism into Camus's portrait of men and women that is almost completely foreign to his previous writings. Up to this time in his experiment Camus insisted upon the innocence of the individual. Guilt was always an outside force found either in the natural injustice of the world or in the evil of false ideas. In *La Chute*, Clamence leads us to believe that suffering is more self-imposed than it is caused by any external factor. This almost totally pessimistic portrayal of us as creatures of both good and evil, whose bad faith can destroy even the best intentions, seemingly introduces a new concept into Camus's thought. But it too can be seen as an extension rather than a negation of his earlier ideas. The universe of *L'Etranger* and the society of *La Peste* are not rejected, but the novels' tension results from an individual's rather than society's struggle with good and evil.

La Chute then may be the beginning of a new phase of Camus's experiment with life, or it could be a dramatic conclusion. In some ways Camus has led us through a complete cycle of self-evaluation. His concluding vision suggests that if the freedom granted by the absurdity of the world is not controlled and corrected by an ever questioning conscience, it has the potential of leading into the abyss of self-negation and the negation of the world. In a world that demands the active engagement of everyone, the acute introspection of a Clamence could lead to total inactivity and the destruction of all that is good.

But whether *La Chute* is a beginning or an end is an academic question of little consequence. The truth is that we will never know. As Sartre remarked, Camus's early death has forced us to look upon an incomplete body of work as his final testimony. It is futile to romanticize about what might have been, what *Le Premier Homme* could have said. The brutal fact is that there is no future promise. Perhaps that is what Camus was saying all along: the tomorrows that might have been have little or nothing to do with the today that is. And it is "the today" that is Camus's passionate concern.

His completed work stands as a testimony to a man who was profoundly concerned with his times. His thought progressed from a personal involvement with the universe to an understanding of it that is acceptable on human terms. It is the human element that consistently informs Camus's thought, prohibiting a strictly systematic approach to any individual piece of his writing. We have said that Camus thinks aloud through his writings, and just as thought is a constantly evolving process, so too is his experimental philosophizing. His philosophy never attains completion, but like Clamence, Camus recognized that he lived in a time when there can never be completion. The best that one can do is to remain faithful to those values one knows are true. Those few issues that Camus illuminated for our times have broadened our range of sympathies and our consciousness of what goes on around us. He has made us see and appreciate "the beautiful face of the world" and taste the richness of life. Life is more interesting and more worth the living than it would have been without his work. Like the great artists before him, he has helped to create the myths by which we live.

Notes and References

Preface

    1. "The Wind at Djémila," trans. Ellen Conroy Kennedy, in *Lyrical and Critical Essays* (New York: Knopf, 1968), 76, 77.

Chapter One

    1. "Create Dangerously," in *Resistance, Rebellion, and Death,* trans. Justin O'Brien (New York: Knopf, 1961), 266.
    2. For a detailed presentation and a clear analysis of Camus's journalistic writings, see Emmett Parker, *Albert Camus: The Artist in the Arena* (Madison: University of Wisconsin Press, 1965).
    3. Letter to author, 3 December 1951. The French text is: "L'histoire du MALENTENDU a été lu reellement dans un journal. Je l'ai introduit dans L'ETRANGER parce j'avais l'intention, en effet, d'en faire une pièce. De même que vous avez remarqué à juste titre qu'il est question de L'ETRANGER dans LA PESTE. Il s'agit là, non d'une petite mystification, mais une manière d'indiquer à de très rares lecteurs attentifs que, dans mon esprit au moins, mes livres ne doivent pas être jugés un à un, mais dans leur ensemble et dans leur déroulement."
    4. *The Myth of Sisyphus,* trans. Justin O'Brien (New York: Knopf, 1955), 18. All succeeding page references are to this edition.
    5. I am indebted to Germaine Brée's, John Cruickshank's, Herbert Lottman's, and Philip Thody's studies on Camus for most of the biographical information contained in this book.
    6. "On Jean Grenier's *Les Iles,*" trans. Ellen Conroy Kennedy, in *Lyrical and Critical Essays,* 328.

Chapter Three

    1. *The Stranger,* trans. Stuart Gilbert (New York: Vintage Books, 1959). All succeeding page references are to this edition.
    2. *Caligula,* trans. Stuart Gilbert, in *Caligula and Three Other Plays,* (New York: Knopf, 1958), 8. All succeeding page references are to this edition.

Chapter Four

    1. "On the Future of Tragedy," trans. Ellen Conroy Kennedy, in *Lyrical and Critical Essays* (New York: Knopf, 1968). All succeeding page references are to this collection.

2. The factual information pertaining to the production of Camus's plays is taken from John Cruickshank, *Albert Camus and the Literature of Revolt* (New York: Oxford University Press, 1960).

3. *The Misunderstanding* trans. Stuart Gilbert, in *Caligula and Three Other Plays* (New York: Knopf, 1958), 105. All succeeding page references are to this collection.

Chapter Five

1. *The Plague,* trans. Stuart Gilbert (New York: Knopf, 1948), 61. All succeeding page references are to this edition.

2. Camus calls *La Peste* a *chronique* to distinguish it from a *roman* or "novel" in the usual sense of the word. The objective narration of the chronicle not only prevents the readers from total identification with the characters and the situations, but it also makes them more receptive to the symbolic implications of the work.

3. Camus writes:

Yes, if it is a fact that people like to have examples given them, men of the type they call heroic, and if it is absolutely necessary that this narrative should include a "hero," the narrator commends to his readers, with, to his thinking, perfect justice, this insignificant and obscure hero who had to his credit only a little goodness of heart and a seemingly absurd ideal. This will render to the truth its due, to the addition of two and two its sum of four, and to heroism the secondary place that rightly falls to it, just after, never before, the noble claim of happiness. It will also give this chronicle its character, which is intended to be that of a narrative made with good feelings—that is to say, feelings that are neither demonstrably bad nor overcharged with emotion in the ugly manner of a stage-play. (126)

4. "Remarque sur la révolte" in *Essais,* ed. Roger Quilliot (Paris: Gallimard, Bibliotheque de la Pléiade, 1965), 1692. All succeeding page references are to this edition.

5. Cruickshank, *Albert Camus,* 178.

6. See Parker, *Albert Camus,* for a thorough discussion of Camus's editorial writing.

Chapter Six

1. Preface to *Caligula and Three Other Plays.*

2. *Actuelles I, Chroniques 1944–1948* (Paris: Gallimard, 1950), 242. All succeeding page references are to this edition.

3. *State of Siege,* trans. Stuart Gilbert, in *Caligula and Three Other Plays,* 171. All succeeding page references are to this collection.

4. *The Just Assassins,* trans. Stuart Gilbert, in *Caligula and Three Other Plays,* ix. All succeeding page references are to this collection.

5. *Actuelles II, Chroniques 1948–1953* (Paris: Gallimard, 1953), 23.

6. *The Rebel,* trans. by Anthony Bower (New York: Vintage Books, 1958), 171. All succeeding page references are to this edition.

Chapter Seven

1. Philip Thody, *Albert Camus, 1913–60* (London: Hamish Hamilton, 1961), 139–40.

2. Hermann Hesse, *Steppenwolf,* trans. Joseph Mileck and Horst Frenz (New York: Bantam Books, 1963).

3. Thody, *Albert Camus.*

4. Ibid., 147.

5. Ibid., 148.

6. Nicola Chiaromonte, "Sartre versus Camus: A Political Quarrel," in *Camus,* ed. Germaine Brée (Englewood Cliffs, N.J.: Prentice-Hall, 1962), 35.

7. Chiaromonte, "Sartre versus Camus," 34.

8. Cruickshank, *Albert Camus,* 126.

9. See Cruickshank's and Parker's studies on Camus for a thorough discussion of the Camus-Sartre debate.

10. Jean-Paul Sartre, "Tribute to Albert Camus," in *Camus,* ed. Brée, 174.

Chapter Eight

1. Preface to *La Ballade de la géôle de Reading,* by Oscar Wilde (Paris: Falaize, 1952).

2. "The Artist and His Time," in *Resistance, Rebellion, and Death,* 266.

3. *The Fall,* trans. Justin O'Brien (New York: Knopf, 1957), 29. All succeeding page references are to this edition.

4. Camus specifically refers to 1955 as a year that is particularly suited for the birth of a new age of tragedy, "On the Future of Tragedy," 298.

5. Mark Twain, "A Fable," in *The Complete Short Stories of Mark Twain,* ed. Charles Neider (Garden City, N.J.: Hanover House, 1957), 599.

6. Aspects of contemporary life that Camus mentions range from the historical facts of World War II to the mundane activities of tourism.

7. *The Fall,* 5, 40, 90, 128, 146.

8. Mme Albert Camus, interview with author, Paris, spring 1964.

9. C. R. Morey, *Christian Art* (New York: W. W. Norton, 1958).

10. A predella depicting Hell was lost before 1550.

11. The iconography of the interior of the altarpiece is both problematic and contradictory. For a detailed discussion of these problems, see Erwin Panofsky, *Early Netherlandish Painting: Its Origins and Character,* 2 vols. (New York: Harper, 1971), 1:212–32.

12. Although much experimentation must have preceded the creation of the Ghent Altarpiece, it is considered one of the first paintings rendered in oil.

13. According to Panofsky, *Early Netherlandish Painting,* 214, "All other All Saints pictures . . . either keep to the text of the *Golden Legend,* and in this case the Virgin Mary is enthroned alone on the right of the Lord while the space on His left remains vacant and the Baptist is relegated to his place at the head of many elders and venerable fathers; or they depart from this text under the influence of the Last Judgment, and in this case the Virgin Mary and the Baptist are symmetrically placed on either side of the Lord but are depicted kneeling instead of enthroned."

14. The inscription is in Latin: "Hic est Baptista Johannes, maior homine, par angelis, legis summa, evangelii sacio, apostolorum vox, silencium prophetarum, lucerna mundi, domini testis."

15. See Panofsky, *Early Netherlandish Paintings,* 95, for a detailed discussion of the Van Eycks' portrait technique.

16. F. O. Matthiessen, *The James Family* (New York: Knopf, 1947), 318.

17. Panofsky, *Early Netherlandish Painting,* 217.

18. "The Wager of Our Generation," in *Resistance, Rebellion, and Death,* 184.

19. "Create Dangerously," 199.

Chapter Nine

1. *Exile and the Kingdom,* trans. Justin O'Brien (New York: Knopf, 1958), 24. All succeeding page references to the stories in this collection are to this edition.

2. At this time Camus was working on an adaptation of Faulkner's *Requiem for a Nun.*

3. Albert Maquet, *Albert Camus: The Invincible Summer,* trans. Herma Briffault (New York: Braziller, 1958), 196–97.

Selected Bibliography

The following list of Camus's writings provides a selected bibliography of his published works. Primary works are cited chronologically.

PRIMARY WORKS

Collected Writings

Oeuvres complètes de Camus, ed. Roger Grenier. Paris: Club de L'Honnète Homme:
  L'Etranger; Le Mythe de Sisyphe; Caligula, 1983
  La Peste; L'Etat de siège; Les Justes, 1985
  L'Homme révolté; L'Eté, 1983
  La Chute; L'Exil et le royaume; Réflexions sur la guillotine, 1984
  Lettres à un ami allemand; Actuelles 1; Actuelles 2, 1984
  Carnets, 1984
  Journaux de voyage; L'Envers et l'endroit; Noces, 1984
  Discours de Suède; Les Esprits; La Dévotion à la croix, 1984
  Les Possédés; Correspondance avec Jean Grenier, 1984.
Théâtre, récits, nouvelles, ed. Roger Quilliot. Paris: Gallimard, Bibliothèque de la Pléiade, 1962.
Essais, ed. Roger Quilliot. Paris: Gallimard, Bibliothèque de la Pléiade, 1965.
Carnets: Mai 1935-février 1942. Paris: Gallimard, 1962. Translated by Philip Thody. New York: Knopf, 1963. Reprint. New York: Harcourt, Brace, 1978.
Carnets II: Janvier 1942-mars 1951. Paris: Gallimard, 1964. Translated by Philip Thody. New York: Knopf, 1965.
Cahiers I: La Mort heureuse. Paris: Gallimard, 1971. Translated by Richard Howard. New York: Knopf, 1972.
Cahiers II: Le Premier Camus. Paris: Gallimard, 1973. Translated by Ellen Conroy Kennedy. New York: Knopf, 1976.
Cahiers III: Fragments d'un combat, 1938–1940. Paris: Gallimard, 1978.

Major Works

L'Envers et l'endroit. Algiers: Charlot, 1936. Reprint with preface. Paris: Gallimard, 1958, 1986. Translated by Ellen Conroy Kennedy. New York: Knopf, 1968.

Noces. Algiers: Charlot, 1938. Reprint. Paris: Gallimard, 1947, 1972. Translated by Ellen Conroy Kennedy. In *Lyrical and Critical Essays.* New York: Knopf, 1968. Reprint. New York: Random House, 1970.

L'Etranger. 1942. Reprint. Paris: Gallimard, 1970, 1972, 1982. Translated by Stuart Gilbert. New York: Knopf, 1946. Reprint. New York: Vintage Books, 1954, 1955, 1956, 1957, 1958, 1959.

Le Mythe de Sisyphe. 1943. Reprint. Paris: Gallimard, 1970, 1985. Translated by Justin O'Brien. New York: Knopf, 1955.

Lettres à un ami allemand. Paris: Gallimard, 1945. (The first two of the four letters were published in 1943 and 1944 respectively.) Translated by Justin O'Brien. In *Resistance, Rebellion, and Death.* New York: Knopf, 1961. Reprint. New York: Random House, 1974.

Le Malentendu and *Caligula.* 1944. Reprint (rev. ed.). Paris: Gallimard, 1958, 1972. Translated by Stuart Gilbert. New York: Knopf, 1958. Reprint. New York: Random House, 1962.

La Peste. 1947. Reprint. Paris: Gallimard, 1972. Translated by Stuart Gilbert. New York: Knopf, 1948. Reprint. New York: Random House, 1965, 1972.

L'Etat de siège. Paris: Gallimard, 1949. Translated by Stuart Gilbert. New York: Knopf, 1958.

Les Justes. 1950. Reprint. Paris: Gallimard, 1973. Translated by Stuart Gilbert. New York: Knopf, 1958.

Actuelles I (1944–48), II (1948–53), III (1939–58). Paris: Gallimard, 1950, 1953, 1958, 1977. Partially translated by Justin O'Brien. In *Resistance, Rebellion, and Death,* New York: Knopf, 1961. Reprint. New York: Random House, 1974.

L'Homme révolté. 1956. Reprint. Paris: Gallimard, 1970. Translated by Anthony Bower. New York: Vintage Books, 1958.

L'Eté. Paris: Gallimard, 1954. Translated by Ellen Conroy Kennedy. In *Lyrical and Critical Essays.* New York: Knopf, 1968. Reprint. New York: Random House, 1970.

La Chute. 1956. Reprint. Paris: Gallimard, 1972. Translated by Justin O'Brien. New York: Knopf, 1957. Reprint. New York: Random House, 1963.

L'Exil et le royaume. 1957. Reprint. Paris: Gallimard, 1972. Translated by Justin O'Brien. New York: Knopf, 1958. Reprint. New York: Random House, 1965.

"Réflexions sur la guillotine." In *Réflexions sur la peine capitale.* 1957. Reprint. Paris: Calmann-Lévy, 1978. Translated by Justin O'Brien. In *Resistance, Rebellion, and Death,* New York: Knopf, 1961. Reprint. New York: Random House, 1974.

Discours de Suède. Paris: Gallimard, 1958. Translated by Justin O'Brien. New York: Knopf, 1958.

Journaux de voyage. Edited by Roger Quillot. Paris: Gallimard, 1978. Translated by Hugh Levick. In *American Journals.* New York: Paragon House, 1987.

Adaptations and Translations

Thurber, James. *The Last Flower (La Dernière Fleur).* Translated by Camus. Paris: Gallimard, 1952.

La Barca, Calderón de. *La Devoción de la cruz (La Devotion à la croix).* Translated by Camus. Paris: Gallimard, 1953.

Larivey, Pierre de. *Les Esprits.* Adapted by Camus. Paris: Gallimard, 1953.

Buzzati, Dino. *Un Caso clinico (Un Cas intéressant).* Adapted by Camus. Paris: Gallimard, 1956.

Faulkner, William. *Requiem for a Nun (Requiem pour une nonne).* Adapted by Camus. Paris: Gallimard, 1956.

Vega, Lope de. *El Caballero de Olmedo (Le Chevalier d'Olmedo).* Translated by Camus. Paris: Gallimard, 1957.

Dostoevski, Fyodor. *Besy (Les Possédés).* Adapted as a play by Camus. 1959. Reprint. Paris: Gallimard, 1971. Translated by Justin O'Brien. New York: Knopf, 1960. Reprint. New York: Random House, 1964.

Prefaces

Chamfort, Nicolas Sébastien Roch de. *Maximes et anecdotes.* Monaco: Dac, 1944.

Salvet, André. *Le Combat silencieux.* Paris: Editions France-Empire, 1945.

Clairin, Pierre-Eugène. *Dix estampes originales.* Paris: Rombaldi, 1946.

Char, René. *Feuillets d'Hypnos.* Paris: Gallimard, 1946.

Leynaud, René. *Poésies posthumes.* Paris: Gallimard, 1947.

Mèry, Jacques. *Laissez-passer mon peuple.* Paris: Editions du Seuil, 1947.

Héon-Canonne, Jeanne. *Devant la mort.* Paris: Siraudeau, 1951.

Mauroc, Daniel. *Contre-amour.* Paris: Editions de Minuit, 1952.

Wilde, Oscar. *La Ballade de la géôle de Reading.* Paris: Falaize, 1952.

Guilloux, Louis. *La Maison du peuple, suivi de Compagnons.* Paris: Grasset, 1953.

Rosmer, Alfred. *Moscou sous Lenine: Les Origines du communisme.* Paris: Editions de Flore, 1953.

Bieber, Konrad. *L'Allemagne vue par les écrivains de la résistance française.* Genève: Droz, 1954.

Targuebayre, Claire. *Cordesen-Albigeois.* Toulouse: Plon, 1954.

L'Etranger. Edited by Germaine Brée and Carlos Lynes, Jr. New York: Appleton-Century-Crofts, 1955.

Du Gard, Roger Martin. *Oeuvres complètes.* Paris: Gallimard, 1956.

Faulkner, William. *Requiem pour une nonne.* Paris: Gallimard, 1957.

La Vérité sur l'affaire Nagy. Paris: Plon, 1958.
Grenier, Jean. *Les Iles.* Paris: Gallimard, 1959.

Uncollected Essays; Collaborations

"L'Intelligence et l'échafaud." In *Confluences* 3, nos. 21–24 (July–August 1943). Edited by J. Prevost. Contains articles on the novel by Valèry, Arland, Prevost, et al.
"Remarque sur la révolte." In *L'Existence.* Edited by Jean Grenier. Paris: Gallimard, 1945.
"Rencontres avec André Gide." In *Hommage à André Gide,* special issue of *Nouvelle Revue Française.* Paris: Gallimard, November 1951.
"Herman Melville." In *Les Ecrivains célèbres.* Edited by Raymond Queneau. Paris: Mazenod, 1953.
Désert vivant: Images en couleurs de Walt Disney. Paris: Société Française du Livre, 1954. Done with Marcel Aymé and Louis Bromfield.

SECONDARY WORKS

Bibliographies

Alden, D. W., ed. *Bibliography of Critical and Biographical References for the Study of Contemporary French Literature.* New York: Stechert-Hafner, 1949–.
Archambault, Paul J. "Camus in Purgatory: Some Recent Scholarship." *Papers on Language and Literature* 9, no. 1 (Winter 1973):95–110.
Beebe, Maurice. "Criticism of Albert Camus: A Selected Checklist of Studies in English." *Modern Fiction Studies* 10, no. 3 (Autumn 1964):303–14.
Bollinger, Renate. *Albert Camus: Eine Bibliographie der Literatur über ihn und sein Werk.* Cologne: Greyen Verlag, 1957.
Crepin, Simone. *Albert Camus: Essai de bibliographie.* Brussels: Commission Belge de Bibliographie, 1960.
Fitch, Brian T., and Hoy, Peter C. *Albert Camus: Essai de bibliographie des études en langue française consacrée à Albert Camus (1937–1970).* Calepins de Bibliographie series. Paris: Lettres Modernes, 1972.
Hoy, Peter C. *Camus in English.* Wymondham, England: Brewhouse Press, 1968.
Roeming, Robert F. *Camus: A Bibliography.* Madison: University of Wisconsin Press, 1968.

Book-length Studies in English

Brée, Germaine. *Camus.* Rev. ed. New Brunswick, N.J.: Rutgers University Press, 1961. An especially informative study. The author had access to

Camus's notebooks while he was still alive, and her use of this material gives the book a special biographical value.

Cruickshank, John. *Albert Camus and the Literature of Revolt.* New York: Oxford University Press, 1960. A comprehensive literary and philosophic analysis of Camus's writings.

Hanna, Thomas. *The Thought and Art of Albert Camus.* 1958; reprint, Chicago: Gateway, 1969. A clear study of the evolution of Camus's thought and art.

Lazere, Donald. *The Unique Creation of Albert Camus.* New Haven: Yale University Press, 1973. A clearly written analysis of Camus's works. A particular emphasis on the penetration of Camus's thoughts into the United States.

Lottman, Herbert R. *Albert Camus: A Biography.* Garden City: Doubleday, 1979. An extensive biography based upon interviews with Camus's family and associates. There is little critical assessment of Camus's work.

O'Brien, Connor Cruise. *Albert Camus of Europe and Africa.* New York: Viking, 1970. Emphasis on Camus's psychological relationship to North Africa and the significance of this relationship to his writings.

Parker, Emmett. *Albert Camus: The Artist in the Arena.* Madison: University of Wisconsin Press, 1965. An interesting analysis and a thorough bibliography of Camus's editorial writing.

Quilliot, Roger. *The Sea and Prisons: A Commentary on the Life and Thought of Albert Camus.* Translated by Emmet Parker. University: University of Alabama Press, 1970. An interesting and extensive revision of one of the earliest and most informative studies of Camus, originally published in Paris by Gallimard in 1956.

Thody, Philip. *Albert Camus: 1913–1960.* London: Hamish Hamilton, 1961. Reprint. New York: Macmillan, 1962. An analysis of Camus's work and a thorough study of his critical reception in England, France, and the United States.

Journals and Collections

The following journals or collections were exclusively devoted to Camus studies. By 1966 there were over twenty-five hundred articles and books on Camus. Since that date he has continued to be among those writers with the most scholarly studies.

Brée, Germaine, ed. *Camus: A Collection of Critical Essays.* Englewood Cliffs, N.J.: Prentice-Hall, 1962. Written by outstanding critics, these essays give an historical perspective to the critical writing done on Camus. The collection contains a translation of Jean-Paul Sartre's "Explication of *The Stranger.*"

Gay-Crosier, Raymond, ed. *Camus 1970.* Sherbrooke, Quebec, Canada: CELEF, 1970. A transcript of the University of Florida conference, 29–30 January 1970. Essay subjects cover the range of Camus's works and the problems they present to the critic.

Gay-Crosier, Raymond, ed. *Camus 1980.* Gainesville: University of Florida Presses, 1981. A retrospective view of Camus's writings twenty years after his death. Major critical thought by some of the world's leading Camus scholars.

Suther, Judith D., ed. *Essays on Camus's "Exile and the Kingdom."* University, Miss.: Romance Monographs, 1981. Essays dating from 1958 to 1973 on Camus's collection of short stories. Excellent introduction and annotated bibliography. Many of the essays have not previously been available to the English-reading public.

Zyla, Wolodymyr T., and Aycock, Wendell M., eds. *Albert Camus's Literary Milieu: Arid Lands.* Proceedings of the Eighth Annual Comparative Literature Symposium at Texas Tech University, 22–24 January 1975. Lubbock: Texas Tech University, 1976. The collection contains essays by some leading American scholars on Camus's art and thought. Excellent introduction to varied critical approaches to his work.

Articles

Girard, René. "Camus's Stranger Retried," *PMLA,* 79 (December 1964):519–33. Reprinted by Materials Center, New York: MLA, January 1966. Named outstanding article published in *PMLA* during 1964–65. Girard convincingly argues that in *L'Etranger,* Meursault does not realize how far-reaching the evil of judgment is. He thinks he is outside of judgment because he condemns those who condemn. In *La Chute,* however, Clamence knows that he is involved in evil, for evil results from a personal pride, which, since it condemns others, condemns itself. According to Girard, the two heroes may be viewed as one. Meursault-Clamence first pictures himself as the victim of a judicial error, but he finally realizes that the sentence is just, because the self can give only a grotesque parody of justice.

Fortier, Paul A. "The Symbolic Decor of 'The Guest.' " *French Review* 46, no. 3 (February 1973):535–42; and "The Creation and Function of Atmosphere in 'The Renegade.' " *PMLA* 88, no. 3 (May 1973):484–95. Both articles translated by Jospeh G. Morello in *Essays on Camus's "Exile and the Kingdom."* edited by Judith D. Suther, 203–15; 217–45. University, Miss.: Romance Monographs, 1981. In these essays Fortier develops his theory that Camus's descriptive passages in the two short stories reflect a meaning that contributes to the stories' actions, characters, and overall sense. The article on "The Guest" focuses on the story's numerous descriptions of nature; the article on "The Renegade" emphasizes the text's atmosphere. In these essays Fortier derives his textual interpretations from a close analysis of definitive descriptive passages.

Jerry L. Curtis. "Alienation and the Foreigner in Camus's *L'Exil et le royaume.*" *French Literature Series* [University of South Carolina] 2 (1975):127–38. After distinguishing vertical (metaphysical) from horizontal (physical) estrangement, Curtis discusses horizontal alienation in the short stories: for Janine horizontal alienation shocks her into vertical alienation; the renegade remains alienated on both levels; whereas d'Arrast resolves the alienation within himself through his fraternity with others. Curtis concludes that Camus's true heroes are consciously reintegrated into themselves and their world.

Brian T. Fitch. "Camus' Desert Hieroglyphics." In *Albert Camus' Literary Milieu: Arid Lands,* Lubbock: Texas Tech University, 1976, 117–31. Fitch distinguishes between the geographic and the metaphoric image of the desert. For Camus the metaphoric desert results from the awareness of a meaningless universe. The two images merge in the act of literary creation: the blinding whiteness of the desert landscape and the writer's white sheet of paper. A writer's solitude and the asceticism writing imposes make the experiences analogous.

B. F. Stoltzfus. "*Caligula's* Mirrors: Camus's Reflexive Dramatization of Play." *French Forum* 8 (January 1983):75–86. According to Stoltzfus, in literature the mirror functions as a metaphor for literariness because it destabilizes all realistic points of reference. Caligula himself destabilizes reality by looking at reflections in the mirror, by reversing the priority of values, and by studying the duplicity mirrored in the eyes of his audience. Stoltzfus suggests that Caligula is the consummate artist whose failure Camus wishes us to understand. Caligula is committed to truth but not to humanity. Like a mirror he distorts reality. He explores the boundaries of the permissible in order to test the limits of the possible, but his experimental revolt ultimately fails, for he does not recognize that rebellion postulates that there is something in life worth rebelling for.

David B. Parsell. "Aspects of Comedy in Camus' *Le Malentendu.*" *Symposium* 37 (Winter 1983):302–17. Parsell presents an interesting and well-documented discussion of Camus's inexplicable involvement with the writing and rewriting of *Le Malentendu.* Parsell convincingly argues that in the early versions of the drama Camus attempted to refute comedy through parody. His later efforts to purify the play by excising the original irony rendered the action more abstract and opaque and consequently violated whatever structural integrity the play had in its original form.

Woolfolk, Alan N. "The Dangers of Engagement: Camus' Political Esthetics." *Mosaic* 17, no. 3 (Summer 1984):59–70. Woolfolk discusses Camus's position on the artist's role in the political arena. Although Camus had unquestioned sympathy for the victims of social injustice and political exploitation, he felt that art did not dictate an involvement in politics. Camus could side with neither the left-wing militants nor the right-wing militarists because each group was prepared to engage in violent actions that would destroy art. According to Woolfolk, Camus exemplifies the anticreedal idealism of a culture that is suffering from a disenchantment with public commitments.

Comparative Essays

Many critical essays on Camus are comparative. As the titles of the following essays indicate, these studies focus on a specific work or a particular aspect of Camus's writings. In general they illustrate either Camus's impact on other national literatures or the influence of these literatures on his writings.

Palmer, R. B. "Dantean 'Figura' in Camus's *The Plague.*" *Journal of Comparative Literature and Aesthetics* 1–2 (1982):53–61. Camus's treatment of history compared to Dante's.

Zagona, Helen. "Reflections in Prison: A Reminder of Verlaine in *L'Etranger.*" *Romance Notes* 25, no. 1 (Fall 1984):35–40. Camus's poetic language compared to Verlaine's.

Bohn, Willard. "The Trials and Tribulations of Joseph K. and Meursault," *Orbis Litterarum: International Review of Literary Studies* 40, no. 2 (1985):145–58. Treatment of Camus's existential hero compared to Kafka's treatment of K in his novel *The Trial.*

Keefer, Frederick T. "Albert Camus' American Disciple: John D. MacDonald's Existentialist Hero, Travis D. McGee." *Journal of Popular Culture* 19, no. 2 (Fall 1985):159–70.

Metzger, Susan M. "Two Points of View on the Absurd: Camus and Claudel." *Claudel Studies* 12, nos. 1–2 (1985):85–89.

Raghavan, Hema V. "To Deny Our Nothingness: The Concept of the Rebel in Beckett and Camus." *Literary Criterion* 20, no. 2 (1985):70–77.

Rea, Joanne E. "Camus' Memory of Joyce's Virag and Athos: Parallels and Transformations." *Revue de Littérature Comparée* 59, no. 3 (July–September 1985):309–11. Sources for the treatment of people in *L'Etranger* traced to James Joyce.

Sarang, Vilas. "Sisyphus and Belacqua: Reflections on Four European Authors." *Chandrabhagal: A Magazine of World Writing* 13 (Summer 1985):57–61. Camus's treatment of the absurd compared to Samuel Beckett's, Kafka's, and Sartre's.

Index